He Was Too Young to Die

A Love Letter to My Friend

Welles Bruce Lobb

ONION RIVER PRESS

Burlington, Vermont

Copyright © 2024 by Welles Bruce Lobb

All rights reserved. No part of this publication may be reproduced, distributed, or transmitted in any form or by any means, including photocopying, recording, or other electronic or mechanical methods, without the prior written permission of the publisher, except in the case of brief quotations embodied in critical reviews and certain other noncommercial uses permitted by copyright law.

Everything in these pages is true. Some names are changed.

Onion River Press
Burlington, VT 05401
info@onionriverpress.com
www.onionriverpress.com

Paperback ISBN: 978-1-957184-59-3

eBook ISBN: 978-1-957184-60-9

Library of Congress Control Number: 2024908334

For Millie, Jeb, and Paul:

May these remembrances of your good son and good brother bring you a richer understanding of Bob, and how his high ethic and honorable passage through life continue to inspire us.

"You can't ignore the dangers of long-distance hiking, but you also can't not do this." – *Momma Llama* from *THRU: An Appalachian Trail Love Story*, by Richard Judy

Robert James Brugmann (1956-1973) was a dreamer and achiever. Had he lived, he might have changed the world.

Table of Contents

Foreword — 7
Introduction — 9

Three Kids

1. New Hampshire — 15
2. Boy Meets Girl — 23
3. Our Big Scary Amazing School — 30
4. My Walking World — 34
5. Bobby B — 37
6. Scout & Wander Boy — 39
7. Into the Wild — 45
8. Appalachian Trail — 48
9. Camp Brugmann — 54
10. Appalachian Trail, Part II — 57

School Daze

11. America's Game — 63
12. Westward Ho — 66
13. Sophomore Slide — 71
14. Steppingstones to Georgia — 76
15. Growing Pains — 79
16. Personality Spectrum — 84
17. Farther & Wider — 88

Wind Shifts

18. Ten Singing Nuns — 97
19. Beast of Beauty & Burden — 102
20. Bob & Me: The Last Waltz — 109
21. Just Guts — 113
22. Brotherly Love — 117

Rollout

23. Springing Ahead — 125
24. Maine to Georgia: Then & Now — 131

25. Late Out of the Gate — 135
26. Plans B & C — 139

Circumstances Beyond His Control

27. Katahdin to Washington to Moosilauke — 145
28. The Right Turn Not Taken — 150
29. The Night Before — 154
30. Lost in the Flood — 157
31. In Bob's Defense — 161

Life Goes On

32. July 4-5, 1973 — 165
33. Back In School — 170
34. Cherie & Joe & Carole & Joel — 174
35. New Journeys — 179

Family Business

36. Millie's Little Red House — 191
37. Paul Brugmann — 201
38. Anna Brugmann & Rashad Brugmann — 207

Back to the Garden (State)

39. Nowhereland — 213
40. Changes — 217
41. Trail Town — 221

Reconstruction

42. Clarendon Gorge — 227
43. The Comeback Trail — 231
44. Green Mountain State — 236

Afterword — 243
Truths of the Trail — 247
Trail Talk — 249
Trail Talk II: Who's Who — 252
Our Old School — 253
Acknowledgements — 255

Foreword
Ryegate, Vermont; July 2023

On the fiftieth anniversary of her son's accident, Millie Curtis tended to her dogs and attended a holiday picnic hosted by friends. Theresa and I accompanied Millie to the gathering, challenged to keep pace in our car with this spunky senior, who zips as any local would at forty-plus down these rubbly country roads. At close to 90, Millie is nowhere near ready for the rest home. But as she, my wife, and I all acknowledged, this was a somber day, a half-century since Bob's fall.

The weather didn't help. A week of rain had turned the state's mountain brooks into unruly torrents, with more and worse to come. It reminded me uncannily of the same timeframe in 1973 and was deeply troubling.

If Millie had these thoughts, she kept them silent. Nor did she say if any news organization had run a story about Bob and the deadly '73 flooding. Her friends, a cross-section of Border Collie people, artists and artisans, and summer residents, know the backstory of how she came to live here, in the Upper Connecticut Valley, but aren't inclined to bring it up. They seemed but mildly interested when I spoke of my history with Millie's son long ago back in New Jersey.

In any event, 105 miles away at Clarendon Gorge, hikers by the hundreds will cross the Bob Brugmann Suspension Bridge this summer and next. They will no doubt admire this impressive span, pause to read the plaque that commemorates my friend, and hastily proceed. To where whim and stamina lead them: Maine, Georgia, the next trail shelter, or up the short embankment to their cars.

As I try to piece together this fifty-year-old tragedy from interviews, memory, and aged diary notes from the cozy confines of home, steaming coffee at hand to fire up the brain, it unsettles me to this day that my friend had his life stolen by one misstep in conditions perfectly lined up against him. This young man of limitless potential, of all people, taken before he finished high school!

But back to the present: Was it the rounds of rain, the sad reminders everywhere, or my perception of human indifference that had me down? Whatever thoughts I harbored this Fourth of July reinforced for me things I'll be saying ahead about passage of time: People move on and forget. And with the decline in local news coverage as we once knew it, retrospective stories like Bob's fail more than not to get rightful attention. That too is sad.

Be that as it is, impulses I can't explain called out to me a few years back, and I've brought Bob's story to print. To preserve it, as it so richly deserves, from getting lost in the flood.

Introduction
Northwestern New Jersey; November 2020

We were shit-deep in Covid-19 and a messy national election. In my months-long quest to remain sane by finding safe open-air activities, I selected Buttermilk Falls. Secluded inside New Jersey's great northwest woods, the falls had long been on my visitation "bucket list," they being one of my birth state's most striking natural features. Getting there took some doing, but after a two-mile walk along a gated dirt road inside Delaware Water Gap National Recreation Area, my wife and I reached the eighty-five-foot-tall gusher, milky in color as advertised.

From Buttermilk's base, it was wooden steps, then a marked path up another steep 1.6 miles to the ridgeline of Kittatinny Mountain. Accepting the challenge of the ascent and now leaving the falls behind, Theresa and I huffed and puffed to the ridgeline before continuing left (northbound, towards Maine) on the 2,197-mile Appalachian Trail. In another twenty minutes we reached a rock slab with a fine view west into Pennsylvania. Here we stopped to rest and eat.

I'm sixty-eight years old. A month before I turned fourteen, in 1970, I first hiked this long, mostly level ridge during a four-day backpack trip with a group of boy scouts. A year later with the same troop, we repeated the hike. In August 1972, now sixteen and a high school junior, I passed here once again, this time with a more ambitious explorer-friend, the extraordinary Robert Brugmann.

Memories, as we know, can be untrustworthy; one hike blends into others. Details get blurred or lost. By luck, however, I kept a diary as a teen and had a young journalist's good judgement to record raw hike data: weather, dates, camp locations, trail mileage, names of important landmarks, etc. Today, the moment Theresa and I reached the overlook with the vista to the west, I knew it: I'd been here before.

Now, can I claim with courtroom certainty that fifty-four years ago with the scouts or fifty-two years ago with Bob Brugmann, I sat at this spot to eat a trail lunch? Positively, no: my notes do not precisely identify this location. Nonetheless, I say with full confidence that Bob and I, as well as the troopers and I, were here. It's a stopping point made for hikers. The view is sweet, and the smooth sun-bathed slab invites tired explorers to sit and dwell and gather themselves. I have no doubt Bob Brugmann and I enjoyed a breather and bite of food here. What we talked about, if anything, of course I cannot recall.

Given the tumult of the pandemic and exhaustion of the historic Biden-Trump election, to return to this peaceful place after decades away and recall it in the context of my long-deceased trail companion was a powerful—and cathartic—departure from the daily meat grinder of bad news and demoralizing politics. While it might be stretching things to claim I sensed Bob's presence, my revisit here absolutely shook awake some dormant emotions and triggered a rush of memories and sentiment.

Theresa and I ate apples and energy bars, drank water, and returned to the trail. At the turnoff to the falls, we descended what we'd earlier climbed and hustled back to the car in the waning daylight. Along this darkening gravel road 1,000 feet below the Appalachian Trail, I seized upon an idea: Bob Brugmann's story needs to be remembered and told. And I must tell it, because nobody but I can.

Thus follows a chronicle of Bob's remarkable if abbreviated walk through life, as I lived it aside him and remember it. How he and I merged, diverted, and came together once more.

Part One

Three Kids

1. New Hampshire
Mount Washington; August 1973

Mist: persistent, penetrating, dispiriting. Wind: slapping, cutting, demoralizing. And over there, just a few steps away, stood Jeb, the surviving brother, seemingly unflappable; expressionless, cocooned in an Army/Navy store poncho, boots and socks muddied, ready to push on. I couldn't imagine what the kid was thinking and he wasn't about to say.

As for me, more than anything, I wanted to be done with this... adventure. Far below in the jolly green valley, catching glimpses of ground when the clouds opened, I could practically see a sun-splashed 75-degree New Hampshire morning awakening as tourists flocked to motel pools or filled their tanks before navigating the hairpin turns up the summit Auto Road. Here though, nearly a mile high in the mists, it was already autumn and socked in.

Back home I had stuff to excite me. I'd be a senior at Hunterdon Central High School and cross-country team captain. I'd been seeing Lori since the spring and might further test out the mysteries of love now that I'd soon be driving. My brother, after a gap year of sorts, was departing for college. While he'd been my pal and mentor, Ken's big personality—through which he'd acquired a celebrity status at school and around our town—made him a tall order to follow. With Ken no longer trolling the hallways and dispensing his charms to win over the opposite sex, my own opportunities to garner some social standing were expanding. My identity as "Little Lobb," the timid kid brother, was about to be blown away. Further ahead, in a form yet to be determined, was college and adulthood.

The only way out of these fucking mountains was to walk out. Jeb's proposal was to return to the trail as soon as possible and do the vaunted Presidential Range hike across the White Mountains to honor his older brother. Well, I couldn't turn it down. Their mom, Millie, and her boyfriend Mike were on their way to somewhere else in New England—maybe the coast of Maine. They'd offered us rides to Franconia Notch, site of New Hampshire's famed Old Man of the Mountain rock profile, for what importance that was. All that mattered to Jeb and me was the daunting fifty-two miles ahead; the rugged four-day traverse of this famous chain of alpine peaks.

We had a good hike going before the rain came on day three. Until this trip I'd never been above 1,800 feet on any Appalachian Trail outing in New Jersey, Pennsylvania, New York, or Connecticut. But up here, the Presidential Range spikes to a nose-bleeding 6,288 feet at Mount Washington and tops 5,000 feet at six other peaks. The range exceeds timberline elevation (around 4,800 feet) for a dozen contiguous miles. This is serious business; rated by many Appalachian Trail devotees as second only to godforsaken Maine in overall difficulty when you combine height, elevation gain, roughness, and remoteness. But when the clouds dissipate and the fog clears, the views from the Presidentials can extend from Montreal to the Atlantic

Ocean. They're sensational and worth not only the effort to get here but any attendant scrapes, cuts, and bruises that may result.

For two kids to be up here on their own, especially in these distressing circumstances, it might have been seen as risky. It certainly was bold. Yet for the imperturbable Jeb Brugmann, soon to enter junior year, it was seemingly another day at the office. Jeb wasn't merely a trail-tough lapsed scout; he was a star hiker. Less than a month earlier, the boy had lost his brother, his closest friend. Yet Jeb's response to Bob's death, as it appeared to me, was to button up and keep walking—nothing more, nothing less.

I'd been running track at home and had developed the lungs and hill-climbing wherewithal to attempt the most arduous hiking I'd yet faced. I'd need that training to clamber over these sons of bitches and to keep pace with Jeb, who was christened James and was Bob's next-in-line sibling by nineteen months. Through three days in the Whites, we were on our game. One after another, we lugged bulky backpacks over a cavalcade of peaks named for men I knew little about: Garfield, Lafayette, Clay, et al. The views in the day-one sunshine were as magnificent as any I've ever known. Above tree line in the fragile vegetation zones, National Forest signage informed us this was the same ecology found hundreds of miles north in the Canadian tundra. How very cool!

Through the midpoint of the journey our luck held. Despite being on a busy trail during prime hiking season, Jeb and I found sleeping space in standard AT shelters. Inside these open-faced "lean-to" structures, we lay our bedrolls on the wooden platforms. While it wasn't the Holiday Inn, it was an improvement from a ground tarp inside a tent. We'd covered a perfectly respectable ten and thirteen miles in the two days since Millie and Mike said their goodbyes. We'd already been above timberline several times, up to 5,249 feet on Mount Lafayette. If Jeb was hurting, you couldn't tell from his steely determination and positive disposition, boosted no doubt from the stunning wilderness where Bob had passed just six weeks before.

Both brothers, with whom I'd explored more than 200 miles of the AT since freshman year, were intensely focused hikers. Yet there were contrasts in their builds and dispositions. Of the pair, Jeb was less conversational and structurally smaller than the sinewy ex-football-playing Bob. Off trail, the granny-glasses-wearing Jeb projected the image of a bohemian absorbed in an avant-garde paperback in a city subway. Bob, meanwhile, more assertive and more easily pissed off, might hang posters around school or organize a protest march if he strongly believed in the cause. Jeb would be there with big brother, protesting with passion but not as noticeably angry. Bob, in broad strokes, was a more hands-on, do-it-yourself, get-it-done type of kid while Jeb, absorbed in the minutiae of a task, was a more measured, academic, and research-driven kind of individual. They were similar as brothers, yet different.

Up in the Whites when the subject of his brother came up, as it sometimes did, Jeb did talk though not in soul-oozing, tear-dropping, gut-wrenching terms, but rather in hushed generalities. About the accident and its aftermath. "It was a wrong place, wrong time moment of terrible luck," he'd mutter. "Bob would want this. For me to stay on the trail and finish my hike."

Did we imagine an alternate reality of seeing Bob passing through with his characteristic nod and flash smile? Leaner after two months of hiking, his straight brown hair grown now to over his ears? *Everything's fine, fellas; the news of my accident is all a mistake.* I certainly did. And scores of times since, in dreams, I have revisited variations of this same fantasy.

He Was Too Young To Die

My notes describe the day-three climb out of Crawford Notch as a "doozy." If you stick to the AT route, the Presidential traverse hike extends from Franconia Notch through Crawford Notch to Pinkham Notch. A notch is a topographical variant of a gap (or pass) in a mountain range. Think of a notch as you might a two-sided cutout in an otherwise smooth piece of lumber. Navigating a notch on foot normally entails a long, steep drop, followed by an equally long and steep haul out. Notches are hard. Around the time we arrived at Crawford, at 1,275 feet, so did sheets of rain.

But not to worry. Thanks to Brugmann-esque forward thinking, Jeb had landed us an advance reservation for that night at Mizpah Spring Hut, a grueling 6.4-mile trail and quad-busting 2,525-foot elevation gain ahead. The White Mountains hut system, under the auspices of the Appalachian Mountain Club, were something special. Though a bit of a splurge, these eight rustic yet comfortable high-mountain hostelries have sheltered weary, weather-beaten foot travelers since 1888 with hot meals and a welcome bunk. A perfect place to recuperate, warm up, eat hearty food , and exchange stories with fellow trekkers and the stalwart Williams, Middlebury, and Dartmouth grads who served with great pride as caretakers, or croo. In spite of slashing rain, slippery footing, and the crossing of the wind-buffeted summit of 5,075-foot Mount Monroe before descending to this diminutive Hotel New Hampshire in the sky, the mere fact that we'd eventually reach a dry refuge propelled us up, up, and over some very nasty trail in generally positive spirits.

I recall after a fabulously filling croo-made pancake breakfast, departing the next morning feeling hopeful despite the shitloads of work ahead. The good news was that the day's 19.6-mile marathon hike would end at Pinkham Notch and conclude our adventure. After Mount Washington, where we'd arrive in three hours, it was more or less downhill—except for the two grinding climbs up to Jefferson and Madison. And mercy, mercy, as we set out from Mizpah Spring, streaks of sunshine beamed through the fog, leaving yesterday's dousing little more than a wet memory.

Alas, the fickle sun and fleeting optimism we grooved on at the outset was merely a tease. By Lake of the Clouds, a still significant hop, skip, and 1,276-foot jump in height to Washington's fabled summit, the golden rays that had bathed us briefly dimmed and vanished like an unconsummated love dream; eclipsed—goddammit—by returning gray-white banks of fog and misty rain. But there was nothing we could do about the temperamental alpine weather except soldier on.

Mount Washington was famous for its lofty, highest-in-the-northeast U.S. altitude, its claimed 150-mile view, and its capricious, sometimes lethal, climate. In addition to being a hiking mecca, the mammoth block of granite was tourist-friendly. Accessed by the Auto Road or a creaky antique railway, it is very popular from June to October. When Jeb and I arrived late morning on August 3, 1973, there were two immediate issues. The first was summit fog so dense there was no view; zero. Furthermore, despite nothing to see, the area was swamped with visitors who'd come up the lazy way, spilling out of station wagons and off the train by the dozens. In the present perspective we'd call this shared mountaintop occupation by both the car and foot crowds a culture clash. Back then, it was for us solitude-craving hikers just a big downer. Indeed, the much-anticipated high point of our four-day Presidential traverse hike, reaching 6,288 feet and soaking in the view, turned into the low point. If we lingered here ten minutes, that was enough.

With thirteen more jarring miles to Pinkham Notch and

pushing noon, I looked at Jeb and he back at me. With a shrug, a nod, and few words, we proceeded. Though I couldn't imagine what he was thinking and he wasn't going to talk about it.

◊

Nightfall coming fast and our tanks near E, Jeb and I busted out of the woods at NH Highway 16, victorious if near delirious from exhaustion, and ending possibly my most punishing trail day ever. To illustrate some of the *Gulliver's Travels*-like encumbrances we faced during the battering, rock-bound, 4,000-foot net descent from Washington, I refer mostly to my diary entry:

> "**Leaving behind the gift-shop and restaurant *tourist-trap feel* of the summit, we *passed over or around a bunch more Presidentials*, Clay, Jefferson, Adams, Madison,** *in thick fog and over rough rockslides.* **After Madison (5367')** began our *final long descent on very rough trail with crossings of many mountain streams and muddy terrain.*"

What the entry didn't mention were the 2,300 feet of elevation gained in scattered segments during that jolting descent from Washington. Nor the day's nearly 5,000 total feet gained if you count everything starting from the hut.

Though we couldn't possibly know it then, our two-mile hoof to the finish in the notch *as darkness began to fall* would mark my final walk with a Brugmann family member for forty-three years.

While the four-day, fifty-two-mile White Mountains traverse finally, blessedly, came to rest at Highway 16, our version of a Gulliverian saga had a couple of more lengthy chapters to go. Wearily and almost wordlessly, Jeb and I would endure another twenty-four hours of pure rigmarole, getting by alone on our collective high-school-kid wits.

Unable to get a room in the AMC lodge at Pinkham due to cost or availability, the resolute, forever intrepid Jeb went back to square one. We pitched a tent in some brush off the side of the road, and passed a muggy, showery night of swatting bloodthirsty north woods mosquitoes between nods of ragged sleep. Come morning we packed up and, with thumbs extended, hitchhiked to Boston, covering the 154 miles in six rides. Finally, after an Amtrak to New York and a connecting bus out to Flemington, we were safely at home by nightfall.

Without balloons, cake and candles, or fanfare of any kind, Dad picked us up from the bus, ending five of the most physically demanding and emotionally fraught days of my young life. Refreshed enough if roundly anticlimactic, I ate, showered, and bedded down in clean linens. And slept long and hard.

I once heard this said about adventures that I think is true: They suck while you're doing them. The reward comes later, in the form of a fridge full of food, TV, and fresh clothing to put on.

I was seventeen years and seven days old. Jeb was fifteen going on sixteen. Bob died thirty days before.

Regrettably, my memories of Jeb from this time on fade. Not unlike the roving cabbie in Harry Chapin's ballad "Taxi," my buddy had more fares to collect, mountains to climb, vistas to see, and flights to the sky ahead. He wasn't sticking around the county.

Me? I was thinking I was born to run rather than to hike. And for a long time, that's exactly what I believed… and did. Except for sporadic outings over the next four decades, I wouldn't take to the Appalachian Trail with a clear agenda again until 2010.

2. Boy Meets Girl
Whitehouse, New Jersey; 1972

We were sophomores when we responded to a help-wanted ad and were hired as dishwashers at the Fiddler's Inn out on Highway 22. By "we" I mean me, Bob, and two other pals from the youth fellowship at the local church, Vic and Billy. This was for us our first dip into formal, taxable employment. At $2.25 an hour, the salary the restaurant offered was more than what we'd make for entry-level jobs at McDonald's or Burger King. But as cautioned at our interviews, with the higher wages came greater work-responsibility expectations. Bob had recently turned sixteen; Vic, Billy, and I trailed him by several months.

Fiddler's Inn was past its peak years and tended to draw older patrons who came for the traditional menu favorites like clams casino on a half-shell or the live Maine lobster. The owners, Harold and Hazel Heintzelmann, were hospitality industry veterans dying to unload the place and retire to the Jersey Shore. Their longtime head waitress, Betty, did her best to keep spirits up during ever slower and bleaker nights. Back in the kitchen, where Bob, Vic,

Billy, and I labored, Alex the chef might liven up any shift busy or not with tales of race cars and sex, told with his inimitable Greek-accented flourish.

No surprise, weeknights were agonizingly slow, but the place did still attract respectable crowds on weekends. Shortly after we started our employment, Harold and Hazel, with input from Betty and Alex, decided on a hierarchy for the new kitchen help that was revealed in our shift assignments. They put Bob on the busiest nights, meaning Friday and Saturday. Billy, Vic, and I filled in elsewhere, landing a Saturday with Bob when multiple hands were needed, or other quieter shifts we could manage without him. But wouldn't you know it. As he had already shown friends, family, teachers, and others with his hiking ability, his performance at school, and his bold venture into the vagaries of love at age thirteen, Bob had quickly demonstrated to the restaurant management a superior level of workmanship and maturity. This emerging star among his comparatively ordinary peers had broken from the pack. Even in washing greasy pots and gunky chinaware, Brugmann was in a league of his own.

The work was not glamorous. Despite welcome levity from the stories Alex spun around the kitchen, or some passing pleasantries with Hazel, Betty, and Gary the busboy, we the young dish grunts sweated proverbial bullets. For hours we ran loads of plates, water glasses, cups, saucers, and silverware through a cranky washer machine, wiped down everything that rolled out, and re-racked each piece of clean dishware, glassware, ashtray, and anything else in a handy location for Betty and her helpers to access for fast redeployment in the dining room. The pace in our corner of the kitchen was frantic; the steam billowing from the washer burning hot. We might find ourselves at any time inundated with commercial-size cooking vats to be hand-washed and returned to Alex on the double without a speck of food residue. By the end of a shift, a film of grease coated our faces and hair. Our clothes were soaked in perspiration and smelly water. It wasn't uncommon for any of us to discover a bleeding finger from a cracked empty wine bottle or splotches of red, blistered skin, courtesy of mishandled cooking oil or some spill at the soup station. When at last we mopped the floor and shut off the kitchen lights, we were more than ready to get the hell out of there, go home, and scrub the filth away.

From the beginning of any night to the end, Bob took on and tackled our responsibilities coolly, systematically, and to a higher standard of care and competency. He could do all he was expected, and do it more efficiently, than the rest of us. To illustrate Bob's overarching value to his employer, consider the case of the dirty spoon—or dirty anything. If a customer discovered a spoon, plate, or coffee cup stained, soiled, or smudged and complained to Harold, the cantankerous old boss would waddle back into the kitchen, the object of the complaint in hand, and confront the boys on dish duty with a lecture and glare. Chances were good that this sort of incident occurred on nights when Billy, Vic, or I were working. Harold wisely knew an evening with Bob holding down the dishwasher made for a more fluid and potentially more profitable night in the larger scope of restaurant operations. After all, fewer complaints from customers equate to bigger tips for Betty's crew and a satisfied clientele that is more likely to return and bring their friends.

It was summer, a few months into our employment, when Bob, Billy, Vic, and I arrived for our Saturday shift. Up the back steps and into the kitchen we found, to our surprise, a new worker receiving instruction from Betty on salad and shrimp-cocktail preparations as Alex hovered over the lesson. In a few minutes we were introduced to Lizzie. Apparently, Betty had pulled some strings with the Heintzelmanns as they had agreed to hire their loyal old waitress's exceptionally mature fifteen-going-on-sixteen granddaughter for Saturday help as a pantry girl. Same as the dish crew, Lizzie was heading into her junior year at a school over in the next county past Somerville. And we couldn't have been luckier because she was heavenly.

By now I was turning sixteen and still without much experience with a girl. Other than some playful pecks with church fellowship girls during games like spin-the-bottle, I'd kissed nobody. For sure I'd wanted to date since I started high school—take girls to basketball games, movies, the Dairy Queen, etc. But I hadn't yet leveraged the balls or mustered the charm to pull anything off.

Among the dishwashers, Bob and Vic had tallied some experience. Going back to eighth grade Bob enjoyed the comforts of a steady, a good one too, until she broke things off sophomore year and possibly broke his heart. Vic with his Rod Stewart looks and hairstyle needed no new temptation. He'd found every pleasure he needed, as Rod had with groupies, with a lineup of ski bunnies from our fellowship group who found our buddy's easygoing ways and finesse on the slopes tough to resist. Billy, a chubby, introverted kid, seemed content to get his kicks from smoking grass and tuning out with psychedelic FM radio.

But know this fact: If Lizzie attended our school, Hunterdon Central, I wouldn't have had a chance on earth with her. She was so far out of my reach, it hurt to dream about us pairing off in a dark corner of the dining room at the end of a shift or acting on imaged affections in the parking lot.

And this Lizzie was no dizzy. Already on her list of accomplishments at school were varsity cheering, National

Honor Society, good parts in plays, and straight-A report cards. She talked openly about the guys in her circle: the senior cross-country captain; some brave boy who'd enlisted in the Navy; a hometown valedictorian she'd gotten her mom's OK to visit down at Georgia Tech or Virginia Tech. Jesus, what about boys our age?

Lizzie had these cute dimples, lovely wavy brown hair, perfect teeth, fabulous probing eyes, and a cool, friendly, forward manner that to me (dare I suggest) felt flirtatious. At HCHS, where I'd existed in the margins of the school's popularity circles, girls of her caliber paid boys of my station no attention. So was my mind distorting reality when I sensed that she stood a little close to me while we went about our work duties in the kitchen, hips or arms brushing in the tight quarters? Or that she paid me a surplus of eye contact? Or... was she this confident and free with all guys?

Slim as my chances with her appeared, I wasn't going to let any opportunity, real or imaginary, with this goddess in our midst slip away. Hopefully she was between boyfriends and available to date, should I be so fortunate to snag one. But also critical in determining a courtship strategy, I had to account for the social dynamics at work. Foremost, I wondered about Bob. As the oldest dishwasher, my friend had experience to pull from; poise, and ambitions beyond a twelfth-grade diploma and future employment in a kitchen. The guy was handsome, mannerly, and was going places.

Around too was goddamn Alex. A mid-thirties lothario with a wife and two children, Alex nevertheless pressed his Grecian charms on Lizzie; talking sexy to her in the restaurant pantry or trying to impress the teenage girl with tales of driving his BMW home to work doing ninety-five down Route 22. What additionally made him a threat, if paradoxically, was Lizzie herself, who in her apparent comfort with boys and men of any age, played along with the chef's fantasies, thus helping to fuel their flirty banter. That was, until the end her shift, when she'd promptly cut the shenanigans off and depart for home prim as could be with her sixty-eight-year-old grandmother.

But Bob, I couldn't figure out what his game plan regarding Lizzie was until I realized he didn't have one. Why would he, of all of us hormonal kids, not? Well, there were practicalities. For one thing, dating cost money. In our pre-driving years it involved arranging rides, sometimes with a parent, horrifying as that prospect was. Dating exposed you to the possibility of rejection, conflict with competitors, or unrecoverable embarrassment should you say or do anything your companion found insulting and went silent on you. In other words, going out with girls could be a terrifying exercise that emptied your wallet and left you dissatisfied or even devastated.

What I had to do to win a night out with Lizzie, if I had a chance of one at all, could be defined in six steps. First, get the home phone number. Second, call and have a solid plan to pitch to her. Third, sweat out a reply. Fourth, arrange transportation. Fifth, be ready to pay for everything: food, gas, entertainment. And, finally, hope my performance during our hours together met her standards for a satisfying ending. At minimum, that's what it took.

Brugmann, as I remember him, would want no part in any of this bullshit. Okay, Bob might have gone a little timid after his ex, Cherie Nordstrom, moved on; but mainly he had already outgrown the rituals of teen love. Bigger things occupied his time and brain: student rights, environmental activism, planning and saving for a 2,000-mile hike, and managing our town's recycling program. At work, Bob wasn't paid to impress a girl. So when my friend, without asking, took on the task of scrubbing Alex's gravy-encrusted vats to a shine, and while Harold wasn't around checking on us, I'd sneak back to the pantry and steal a few mid-shift minutes with Lizzie.

Thinking about this a half-century later, I also believe that as an honorable guy and friend Bob sized up my interest in the girl and decided he'd step out. I make this conjecture because he certainly had the social wherewithal to make his own pitch to her, if he wanted to. Bob may have been telling me without saying as much, "She's yours, Bruce. I'll sit this one out."

As one would in the years before there was an internet, I found her parents' number in a telephone book collection in the school library. Going out for cross-country and making varsity had boosted my confidence... *so just make the call.* Say a little prayer too.

We went out twice to a movie and a musical. She was the nicest companion you could imagine. Is celestial too lofty a word to describe how I felt during our hours together? Of course, like most things too good to be true, so was this. On my return trip to reality and assessment of any pathway forward for us, I correctly judged the window for Lizzie and I to dally as romantic partners had closed. That was that.

The Heintzelmanns sold the restaurant and by Thanksgiving the Fiddler's Inn was locked up: lights off, kitchen silent, heat turned back. Alex moved on as itinerant chefs do; Betty retired. Her granddaughter and I exchanged a few more letters and cards until it became pointless. Bob would accomplish great things at school, hike 500 miles of the Appalachian Trail, and be dead by the next July.

Lizzie came to the memorial service. She cried for Bob and kissed me in my grief. I've not seen her since.

3. Our Big Scary Amazing School
Flemington, New Jersey; 1956-70

For the time and place, you couldn't do better than Hunterdon Central for a high school education. I make this assertion even as one who battled from behind all four years to find his lane in the classroom, in sports, or anywhere. As for Bob, though he might gripe about some teacher or school policy on a hike or during a lull at football practice, I credit to a large degree what he experienced here for shaping my bright yet wholly ordinary friend into a teen of exceptional accomplishment.

To understand how that happened, we need to go back, dig around, and take a close look at the old alma mater. So I examined it from the very bones from which it grew, the accident of its locational advantages, and the phenomenal human talent that endowed and sustained it.

Truly, the Central I knew was an anomaly: a large school in both enrollment and landmass with a progressive drumbeat that defied its rural location within one of New Jersey's redder counties. Built in 1956 on vacant farmland just beyond the town line, HCHS replaced the old

Flemington High School. Its creation, driven by anticipated growth, was a consequence of the state's directive to "regionalize" a looser, older education system into one of larger, defined geographic districts. As such, in addition to Flemington, regionalization in Hunterdon County resulted in the closure of three other small town high schools, now morphed into districts called North Hunterdon, Delaware Valley, and South Hunterdon. Without a doubt, due to its leviathan size and other special demographics, Hunterdon Central benefitted most of the four newly formed schools.

Delaware, East Amwell, Raritan, and Readington townships, as well as Flemington borough, would comprise the HCHS district. Together this amounts to a 160-square-mile sending area that spanned the east-west breadth of the county and positioned Central inside the overlapping cultural and media spheres of New York City, Princeton, Trenton, and greater Philadelphia. Major roads, including US 22 and its later interstate companion I-78, ran east to New York; Route 31 south to the capital at Trenton; and US 202 across the Delaware River into Pennsylvania.

One drawback of the new system were the bus rides. If you lived north of Flemington in the sticks of Readington, as Bob and I did, or down south past Ringoes or Rosemont, you could expect a fifty-to-seventy-five-minute trip on a squeaky, rattling, gear-grinding bus each way to school. If you stayed late for sports, clubs, or play rehearsals, schooldays that began before sunup and ended hours after dark were normal. That was the price we paid, I suppose, for the good fortune to attend one of New Jersey's best public high schools.

Arguably the best outcome of the new system was that HCHS got the county seat of Flemington and its encircling, fast-growing township of Raritan. As the seat of local government, historic and prosperous Flemington was a natural draw for professional people to work in law, county administration, the courthouse, and in its modest yet diversified industrial base. This offered good career opportunities for both blue-and white-collar workforces. Surrounding the town and its spillover into Raritan Township were acres upon acres of poultry and dairy farms, as well as scattered small communities and blink-and-miss villages. The area's first modern hospital, Hunterdon Medical Center, opened a mile north of town in 1953 and brought with it scores more of well-educated professionals. Of course Flemington was already widely known for being the site of the 1935 Lindbergh baby kidnapping trial as well as home to the treasured Flemington Fair and Speedway.

When New Jersey's 1960s new-home explosion gained a foothold in Hunterdon's big open spaces, some of the first large-scale subdivisions went up east of town off Route 202, with its access to New York, Philly, and Trenton. While much of the rest of the county would languish as an agrarian backwater for another decade or longer, Flemington and the HCHS district already had a couple of legs up in shedding its farm and small manufacturing-driven provincialism for the vibrancy and affluence of a bedroom community chain-linked to a faster and more urban Jersey to the east.

Not to be overlooked, and unusual for rural New Jersey, Flemington was home to a substantial Jewish population. Drawn there originally by affordable land, poultry production, and the town's agricultural commodities industry, and later by people fleeing Europe's Arian political shadow, Flemington's Jewish community in time would branch out into other areas of the economy, most notably real estate, retail, and sales of luxury goods. I've cited this development for its role in bringing students from prominent families and their cultural traditions into the school, and their elevating influence on student life from stage to sports to service clubs. My belief was that this engaging minority population was a driver in making HCHS a known regional leader in activism, the arts, and forward-thinking administrative decisions.

It was this confluence of demographics and culture which fourteen-year-old Bob and I walked into when we entered Central's plush semi-collegiate Lower House in September of 1970. Beyond a freshmen-only classroom building, the newly open Lower House encompassed individual library, music, PE, and Vo-Tech buildings. It marked Central's first expansion since the school opened fourteen years before. For me, Bob, and scores of other wide-eye bumpkins from the township feeder schools, coming into HCHS was dazzling, opportunistic, and more than a little intimidating.

Ready or not, get used to it.

4. My Walking World
Fanwood, New Jersey; 1956-65

Before I could imagine any school experience beyond diminutive La Grande Avenue elementary; or formed any vision of New Jersey wider than the stops on the train line to New York plus a few shore towns; or really knew much about much of anything, including trails and hiking, I walked.

With my mom, brother, sisters, or uncle, walking was how we got around our tidy, seemingly safe suburban town. Far less so than driving, walking to school, stores, the park, friends' houses, church, the public library, or the grandparents' home was a normal part of life sixty years ago. From the time we started school, Ken, the neighbor kids, and I knew to use sidewalks and how to properly cross streets. By seven or eight, when our walks extended to the next town, Scotch Plains, they became some of my first tastes of adventure and independence. Car travel was reserved for trips to bigger places such as Plainfield and Westfield for shopping or appointments, or the occasional trip to the shore.

Today a fancier word comes to mind for what amounted

to serendipitous kids expanding their understanding of the world. We were *flâneurs* of a kind: curiosity-driven child wanderers who traveled on foot to observe and gain meaning and knowledge in the small things of life. Ken and I took our cues from Uncle Merv, Mom's war-injured older brother, who might have embodied as pure a *flâneur* spirit as anybody I've known. Merv didn't walk around Plainfield to exercise the dog, lose a few pounds, or satisfy some weekly mileage goal. Instead, this unconventional man would return from his strolls down littered avenues or railroad tracks with some quirky, if insightful, observation about local life to share.

Mixed in with my *flânerie*-like peregrinations around Fanwood and Scotch Plains came, courtesy of Dad, my earliest exposures to actual hiking. Two destinations I recall visiting are the trails of the Watchung Mountains nature reservation and a path close to home along a transmission line. "Look here," Dad pointed. "A battle, Revolutionary War, was fought; before that Indians, the Lenni Lenapes, camped and hunted." To convince me, my ex-Eagle scout father would stir up the dirt with his shoe and find an arrowhead or some other buried artifact to add to his collections at home.

One of my most valued mementoes from Dad is a striking photo of him staring at a cascading brook in northwestern New Jersey. In the years between his end of military service and settling down with my mother, Dad was a sort of footloose bachelor who bummed around with pals from Plainfield who enjoyed hiking, camping, and visiting local taverns. Growing up, I saw myself in the young man in the picture and imagined being the roving explorer my father was. The 1949 photo from Van Campens Glen in today's Delaware Water Gap National Recreation Area hangs in my home today. Dad was twenty-six years old, in the prime of life.

Bill Lobb would live to ninety-four and retain a lifelong interest in the outdoors, stemming no doubt from his scouting days and youthful adventuring. But after our short rambles together in my first decade, I couldn't remember him hiking or walking for pleasure. Before he was forty, it seemed, the twin demands of his building business and fatherhood-times-four had effectively consumed him and extinguished any leftover yearnings to head off on foot, look around, maybe bring home a hundred-year-old medicine bottle. Aside from our early escapes into nature, there were no later outdoor bonding experiences or push to join a scout troop; just one camping trip to New England in 1967. Alas it seemed Dad gave up his love of exploring and sunk into domesticity and the duties of a family provider.

What Dad, with an assist from Uncle Merv, had instilled in me is an enduring wonderment for the variety of living things and human imprint you can find when you enter the wilds—the unbuilt upon lands beyond the omnipresent manicured lawns, parking lots, and roadways of our ever-shrinking natural world. So we moved to Hunterdon County in '65, I was taken to a place that seemingly was in my DNA to explore. In that relatively undisturbed environment, fueled by my nine-year-old imagination, I wasted no time getting acquainted with the seasonal discharges of the rivulet that splashed through our yard, the fallow fields behind the house, and the nearby woodlands with their rock walls and overgrown roads into the great beyond. Was there really a hermit's cabin somewhere up on Cushetunk Mountain, as rumored? Was that the mountain's mystery foghorn I heard bellow or some faraway train? For a child who dwelt in the distant corners of his imagination, I had come to paradise.

5. Bobby B
Readington Township, New Jersey; 1968-70

Robert James Brugmann was not privileged or known to be gifted when he arrived in fifth grade with his mother, Millie, who worked in the personnel department at Colgate-Palmolive, and two younger brothers. This was in rural Readington, which at almost forty-eight square miles was the largest municipality by area in the county. Their modest house sat back from Hillcrest Road with a barn and a few acres so Millie could board and exercise her horses. Like many other newcomers to the area, the family migrated from parts east, in their case the rapidly developing suburban towns of nearby Somerset County.

My first memories of Bob date to seventh grade. We played on rival squads in the afterschool basketball league; by eighth grade we were teammates on a school soccer club, the Shin Busters. We were also scuffling musicians. While I played a woeful third trumpet in the band, Bob was a nearly as bad second-part kid up the line. So forgettable a musician he was that no friend I interviewed could recall Bob in this role. A much more polished instrumentalist than us both, however, was the up-and-coming James Eric Brugmann, or Jeb, Bob's younger brother, who earned some notoriety around the band room and concert stage as a horn soloist. Nevertheless, in the next year or two, Bob and I would link up more significantly as our shared interests shifted from playing mediocre sports and inept music to hiking and environmental concerns.

I don't remember Bob in any of my classes. Most likely he had tested into the strongest academic group within our class of 152, an honor from which my lower scores denied. But another memory, tinged with envy, remains clear: Bob and the smart-and-stylish Cherie Nordstrom, one of Readington's best catches, dated throughout eighth grade and stayed a couple going into high school.

The Challenger, our eighth-grade yearbook, lists student council, two choral groups, three sports, band, and two clubs (rocket and photography) as Bob's selection of school activities. His declared ambition: Architect. The graduation program cites Robert Brugmann as co-recipient of the Class of 1970 "Best English Student" award. As the yearbook bio illustrates, despite his low-volume manner Bob was accomplished, goal-oriented, and well-rounded. He was a leader and a scholar, but you didn't necessarily know it because he didn't promote himself as such. Bob just got things done, and people noticed.

By eighth grade we were friendly acquaintances, lunchroom pals you might say, but academic separation, his workload, and the attention he gave his girlfriend would delay our becoming close friends until high school. Ahead of the bonding to come as football teammates at Hunterdon Central, our middle school years were independent of each other, charting our own courses to become future hiking companions.

6. Scout & Wander Boy
Readington; 1968-70

Aligned with his inclination to seek challenge and develop self-reliance, Bob found an avenue to walk when he joined the Boy Scouts of America in 1967. With opportunities to learn practical skills they don't cover in school—for instance, where else could a kid learn how to start a campfire in a snowstorm with a single match when survival depended on that one successful light?—scouting doubtless tapped into some growing desires and helped awaken my friend to the elemental joy of sleeping under the stars and exploring the woods with little else but boots and a rucksack filled with survival supplies.

Around this time, as the nation saw explosive, youth-driven social upheaval, it concurrently underwent a sweeping environmental movement which gave rise to the first Earth Day in April 1970. Both movements, for a new social order and the protection of our endangered planet, would deeply influence this enquiring and conscientious youngster right away and for the remainder of his shortened lifetime.

While Bob and I both would take some satisfaction in

the pieces of environmental legislation that passed in Washington, on the ground back in New Jersey we also bore witness to what can best be described as accelerating ecological destruction of a local variety. With the westward push of Garden State suburbs into our backyards, we watched with growing despair as our cherished woodlands and farms were broken apart and transformed one after another into piles of dirt and rows of cinderblock for new subdivisions and other commercial building startups. As many in the state shrugged off the changeover as an inevitability of the times, or saw it as "progress," freshly minted ecology hawks such as Brugmann and I envisioned a collision course with a coming global disaster. Which, as it turns out, showed us to be quite prescient for fourteen.

Where Bob lived on Hillcrest Road was particularly affected by the proliferation in housing starts. To his east, a mile or so away, lay a massive new development alongside Route 202. To the west, deeper into Readington and Hunterdon County, the dozers too had arrived, but change so far was more scattershot with just handfuls of houses going up here and there.

But in pro-development Branchburg and Bridgewater over the line in Somerset County, farms and open spaces were stunningly rearranged into new communities of cul-de-sacs. Indeed, the surrounding area took on something of a DMZ quality to it as the densely urban and suburban eastern New Jersey lay in sharp contrast to the mostly rural and as-of-yet unspoiled west Jersey.

Luckily, close by in Hunterdon, we had the newly filled Round Valley Reservoir, buttressed by several thousands of acres of protected woods on Cushetunk Mountain to serve as a line of defense against the advancement of the destruction from the east. As much as the economic and population forces that had already maligned much of the state were now pressing against our neighborhoods, we took illusive comfort in having this piece of semi-primordial land at our doorstep the developers couldn't go after with their machinery and turn into yet more houses and parking lots.

My personal experience with New Jersey's changing physical appearance, and how it would influence me to swing green and seek woods, both differed and overlapped with Bob's eco awakening. Despite an early interest in the great outside, scouting never strongly called to me. Due to no real parental push, its geeky vibe, and my own insecurities regarding its core emphasis on individual skill mastery—a core weakness of mine—I didn't see myself as boy-scout material. What I did have in limitless supply, however, was a soaring imagination about wild spaces and places. This powerful curiosity would later serve as my main entry point into the world of trails and nature.

◊

So how did I, no child prodigy, figure out that Planet Earth in the late sixties was in the nascent stages of an environmental collapse? Because as the kid of a central New Jersey homebuilder, I watched it coming with each new subdivision approval, road widening, and shopping center project; starting in fourth grade and lasting throughout high school. Within this span of less than a decade, the county population would jump by a third, with the bulk of the gains in Readington and nearby greater Flemington. We went from boondocks to the next coming of Bridgewater just like that.[1]

Our family arrived in Readington on gravel-surface Dreahook Road in 1965. We'd come from Fanwood,

---

[1] Bridgewater Township transitioned from generally rural in the 1950s to a fully developed bedroom community by the 1970s. Its population from 1950 to 1970 nearly quadrupled. Western Bridgewater extends to within two miles of Readington.

twenty-seven miles to the east, inside the suburban yoke around New York. The universe we'd known there—narrow spaces between houses, traffic, trains, planes, and buses—vanished here, replaced by manure scents from neighboring farms, the evening flights of bats, and nocturnal choruses of singing crickets. One morning we spotted two copperheads coiled in the ditch alongside the road. There were rumors of a foghorn somewhere high up the mountain! I was nine and would ride my first school bus. A displaced suburbanite entranced by the new landscape of fields and country roads to unknown places.

We'd come in the wake of a decision by Dad and Uncle Gene to transfer their work from inner Jersey and bank their financial future on the local building boom. For their planned construction of colonial-style homes on two-acre lots, Lobb Brothers Inc. purchased thirty acres of scrub cedar fields at the foot of the Cushetunk Mountain. First house up was for Uncle Gene, Aunt June, and our three cousins. Next was for us—Mom, a woman of culture facing a bumpy adjustment to a more rustic way of life; Dad; older brother Ken; younger sisters Sally and Nancy; and I. Two or three dozen more Lobb-made domiciles would follow the initial subdivision.

Before this new development would permanently alter the character of the area, I enjoyed great imagination nourishment in the surrounding emptiness. Inside these wilds were two distinct domains to explore: the remaining farmland and the mountain. Bisecting it all was the headwaters of Holland Brook, fed by trickling springs clean enough to dip your face into and sip. To reach these places, I gravitated to the local system of abandoned farm and woods roads and proceeded along them on foot or bike into the deep bush. In my naiveté, I clung to the notion that we'd always have this expanse of land as it was, unviolated by change, for play and discovery. As one might hang onto a belief in Santa Claus or the tooth fairy, I guarded this vision of Eden for as long as I could.

The farmland came in two forms: the disused "successional" fields slowly returning to trees and the active acreage still tilled and planted every spring. All connected by the old tractor lanes that I could access from out the door. The fields seemed vast, offered good exploring, and did in fact stretch a full mile to County Route 523. But, ultimately, it was the mountain that would capture my fancy.[2]

Not a hundred yards from our driveway was a path into the woods at the foot of Cushetunk. In my mind this was the gateway to another dimension. Here, forty miles from Newark, in the most densely populated of the fifty states you could roam for a day and not see another human. Part of the mountain's draw was its distinctive horseshoe shape, encasing the expansive Round Valley beneath Cushetunk's two long ridgeline prongs. At 600 feet higher than the surrounding Jersey midlands, the mountain is visible from numerous angles as many as ten, twenty, or more miles. In a part of the state that lacked interesting natural features, Cushetunk was exceptional. The mountain and its woods slid into my consciousness early, and its beauty little changed today continues to bring me back for hikes and reflection. For a few years, prior to going to high school, escaping here for play was as internalized in my daily life as checking the stats of my favorite New York Mets or protecting myself from Ken's unprovoked bouts of insults and roughhousing.

Alone or with our faithful black and brown Lab, Ozzie, I'd enter the woods, follow one of the old tracks, then another. I might lose my way and be gone for hours. In

---

[2] These fields of my dreams were bulldozed into an exclusive golf and residential development, Stanton Ridge, by the early 1990s.

school I struggled with social and academic insecurities; at home against an angry brother and parents pushed to their breaking point by the pressures to earn a living and tend to the individual needs of their four children. But up here, away from all that, inside my own world I found peace and safety. And the beginnings, I think, of an identity: as a seeker of roads less travelled. That's me, for sure!

7. Into the Wild
North Hero and Cambridge, Vermont; July 1969

A few weeks shy of my thirteenth birthday, the Lobbs went on a rare family vacation to an unlikely destination: Vermont. Prompted by a classified listing in the local paper, Mom and Dad rented a cottage on Lake Champlain from a New Jersey couple who themselves owned a summer residence nearby. During our stay the kindly cottage owner offered to take her teen daughters, Katie and Janet, along with Ken, Sally, and I, into the majestic Green Mountains for a day of hiking to the state's highest peak, Mount Mansfield. We three Lobbs hadn't a clue to what we were about to get into; but tired of swimming in the frigid lake waters, we agreed to go.

Mrs. Wallace bid us goodbye and good luck and left us with a map, sandwiches, and a few sendoff instructions at a roadside location called Smugglers Notch. While she rode the sleek ski gondola to the top, our young quintet would walk the aptly named Long Trail to the summit the tough way: up 2,200 feet of lung-busting elevation gain to Mansfield's lofty height of 4,395 feet above sea level.

As I recall, much of the 2.4 miles up was a punishing, push-the-limits stamina test for courageous little Sally, age 11, and me. Meanwhile, the Wallace sisters and Ken (no doubt seizing the opportunity to impress a pair of girls) took it in stride. As we rose in height the spruce forest gave way to thin, dwarfish birch trees while the wind picked up. It was mid-summer, but as Mrs. Wallace had advised us, pack a jacket; it gets chilly high on the mountain.

Nearing the top, the path became steeper and rougher. At a cliff just below the mountain's anthropomorphically named Chin, a short but precipitous grab-and-tug from pay dirt, Sally and I panicked and stopped. Ken and the girls strode skyward without pause as my sister and I, frozen with fear, waited on a windy ledge below the day's prize. After the trio of successful summiteers returned, raving about the view, the five of us safely descended back to Smugglers Notch and into the car. It was the end of an adventure, but the beginning of something grand and enduring.

Despite my failed attempt to summit the mountain, this was my first real hike, and a whopper at that. There was a personal shame to square with from my caving to acrophobia on the ledge, but there was also new resolve. Back at the cottage and enthralled with the just sampled 272-mile all-Vermont "Footpath in the Wilderness," I thumbed through a mottled edition of the *Guide to the Long Trail* and hatched an idea. Later back at home with tools borrowed from Dad, I entered the brush of Cushetunk Mountain and began to snip and saw the way for my own "long" trail to Round Valley Reservoir.

"Long," of course, is relative. The distance up and over Cushetunk to the reservoir shoreline is around two miles. Still, on many days that summer and fall, I cut a little deeper and higher until a visible pathway took shape in the woods. From previous wanderings here I had a general understanding of the mountain and where to go. But mainly I just followed my innate directional instincts.

Here I was, this nomadic eighth-grade kid flying solo through a fantasyland by handcrafting a path through the woods. Unlikely as it was, I stuck with the job and eventually reached the 837-foot mountaintop. Then continuing down Cushetunk's steep backside, work concluded at the reservoir in March 1970. In seven months of hacking away at poisonous vines, doing battle against bugs and thorny bushes, and sidestepping the occasional snake, I had built a trail!

Construction was amateurish but not without thought. To give my handiwork a sense of permanency, I hammered nails into trees to mark or "blaze" the route. Before it fell into disuse after I started high school, the pathway had briefly thrived as a neighborhood attraction, a stealthy hideaway explored by friends but little known beyond a dozen or so of us. Had it been a scouting project, it was worthy of a merit badge.

8. Appalachian Trail
Northwestern New Jersey; June 1970

As it turned out, the Vermont hike and Cushetunk Mountain trail-building project that followed it were direct launch pads to my first Appalachian Trail experience. George Hill, a friend from Readington School, knew of my interest in hiking and coaxed me into coming with his scout troop on a backpacking trip on the New Jersey AT after our eighth-grade graduation. Going on George's adventure would entail four days of rigorous walking, three nights of camping, and a pre-trip visit to Majors department store for the cheapest sleeping bag and work shoes I could find.

My collective knowledge of the AT was this: It was a twisty line of dashes or dots on the free gas station road maps I had stockpiled and studied. It entered New Jersey at the Delaware Water Gap and traversed its mountainous northwest region. (Which was kind of a joke because everybody said what we in Jersey called mountains were hills.) It was a longer, way longer, extension of Vermont's Long Trail. I'd also heard there were a dozen or so nutcases a year called "thru-hikers" who'd been credited for having completed the entire Maine-to-Georgia trail route. And every so often Dad would mention the trail, having sampled it in spots with pals during his younger days.

What George Hill offered me was altogether new and daunting territory. I'd be hauling thirty pounds of clothing, food, and camping supplies on my back for what I was told was fifty miles; and within the expedition's High Point to Water Gap stretch was one hard-to-imagine nineteen-mile day. Other than some can-do spirit, I had no scout-acquired skills to rely on and would struggle with basics such as securely tying a sleeping bag to the frame of my pack. But I was itching to join George's troop for the hike and not botch things up for them.

Strapping, easygoing George was a fun-loving kid with whom I buddied up at Readington. His troop consisted of boys from local working-class homes, known in the scouting community for being skilled campers. While at first glance they seemed a motley bunch of middle school-age goofballs, these Three Bridges kids were quite focused when it came to the business of earning merit badges for backpacking, wilderness survival, and first aid, among others. George, for all his clowning, was a responsible and dedicated scout. As he wrote in my school yearbook ahead of the hike, "To a fellow camper: good luck on the 60 Miler, if you can make it. I hope you don't! Don't forget your extra underware." [sic]

For the fifty-miler, which George for unknown reasons inflated by ten miles for the yearbook, my fourteen-year-old gym class pal was the troop's de facto third in command behind two adult leaders, Stan and Russ. While I was not a scout in this troop or any, George was able to open doors for me to go as his guest for an adventure whose only rule was, "Don't wimp out!"

According to the maps, the well-travelled High Point to Water Gap portion of the New Jersey AT measured forty miles tops—if you continue alongside I-80 to the bridge to Pennsylvania. Even taking into consideration a few route modifications over the past five decades, there was no way the distance we hiked exceeded forty-one or forty-two miles. However, the troop had touted the journey as being fifty miles (to satisfy the merit badge standard, I believe), so everybody called it that: the fifty-miler.

Our party included ten scouts, the two scoutmasters, and me. Our route followed the Kittatinny Mountain ridgeline and offered us ample views (including a few stunners from fire towers), good camping locations, and enough up and down and rocky footpath to be both a fun and respectably strenuous hike. It challenged us without surpassing our capabilities. On an AT difficulty scale of zero to five, I rated the section 2.9.

Other than the lofty ridge itself, which extends some 200 miles from Pennsylvania to the Hudson River, the most notable natural feature along the mountain in New Jersey is a jewel of a glacial lake known as Sunfish Pond. Once threatened by power companies who coveted its water for electricity production, the pristine forty-four-acre pool was a popular hiking destination and prime camping spot. For us tired scouts it was a landing place worthy to arrive early and enjoy; for hippies and other nature lovers who hiked the gentle four miles up from the Water Gap, an oasis to take off their clothes and party. The pretty little pond made big news a few years before when hundreds of eco-minded citizens, led by Supreme Court Justice William O. Douglas, staged a highly publicized "Save Sunfish" rally there. Unlikely as it might seem in today's polarized political landscape, Thomas Kean, a future Republican governor, jumped into the fight on the environmentalists' side and helped protect the property while appeasing the utilities in a land-swap agreement that spared the pond.

He Was Too Young To Die

To arrive at Sunfish in time to fully embrace the amenities, Stan and Russ knew they'd have to bust our pubescent little fannies the day before to the tune of 18.9 miles from Stokes State Forest to a campsite at Rattlesnake Spring. Outrageous as the idea of asking kids twelve, thirteen and fourteen years old to walk that distance with loaded packs sounds now, half a century ago this was an honorable challenge for a scout to accept. In the end every kid made it, including the whiniest and most out of shape troopers.

Lucky for all, we hit a streak of warm days, cool nights, and no rain. While Stan's and Russ's ambitious itinerary would nearly wipe out half the troop, we managed to hobble 7.6 miles on day three to Sunfish and claim a campsite with a view and opportunity to rejuvenate our parched, dirty selves in the soothing pond waters. As anticipated, the area filled up with AT travelers, other scout groups, and droves of young adults up from the Water Gap. It was a Friday afternoon; time to let loose.

In another stroke of exceptional luck, our friendly camper neighbors happened to be a young woman with her hippie boyfriend. And in a breathtaking moment, the girl dropped her cutoffs and dove off a rock into the water in a string bikini. For us thirteen and fourteen-year-old boys, brain-drained after thirty-six pulverizing trail miles and three days of powdered food and shit sleep, we could only watch her streamlined plunge and imagine things.

Now standard-bearers of PC who might squirm at my inclusion of this magical moment in our story, hear ye: The girl provided, no contest, our best viewing of the trip. An indelible instant of beauty in-the-flesh juxtaposed with nature's gifts. And for eleven electrified kids, a bonus for our efforts to hike the many miles down from High Point.

Furthermore, while I've loved the challenge and rugged aesthetic of the Appalachian Trail from the beginning, I must say it somewhere that the act of hiking it I've found over five and a half decades to be about as lustful as going to the dermatologist. Aside from the Sunfish Pond swimmer, an anomaly never forgotten, few individuals out there give off heat of a sexual kind. Instead, the sense you get from the passing armies of weighted-down trekkers, the thru-hiker types, is they're consumed with covering the daily mileage, eating, managing supplies, and, of course, more eating. Those my age, slower and wiser, are inclined to hide every inch of skin inside suits of synthetic fabrics designed not to bring attention to gym-sculpted body parts, but to repel moisture and safeguard the human machine against (name it) sun, heat, cold, sweat, dirt, snakes, bears, poisonous plants, ticks, and every manner of bug or airborne virus. The scenery the trail offers is of a very different sensory appeal than the variety you find when strolling in the sands on a July afternoon at Seaside Heights.

That's not quite to say that the Appalachian Trail experience is one of universal celibacy. I believe also that within the younger cohort of long-haulers any modesties they bring into the mountains from society soon fall by the wayside, private parts get exposed, and intimacy alfresco as a byproduct of the close contact and invigorating lifestyle follows. In Richard Judy's novel of an AT thru-hike, every hiker but one has a hook up. The frustrated kid who didn't quits halfway and heads for home.[3]

To conclude this salty rumination, I ask: What book worth your effort to read omits sex? I say, no book. Enjoy the diversion, as we kids did. Soon enough we'll circle back to the less salubrious affairs of Bob Brugmann, who was doing important things of his own that summer and walk through his hiking metamorphosis: from scouting to family

---

[3] *THRU: An Appalachian Trail Love Story* (Appalachian Trail Museum, Gardners, PA, 2014)

camping to hitting the trail with me and Jeb.

After swimming, feeding, and viewing a late solstice sunset, the troopers and I that splendid eve rested in the knowledge that we were on the downside of the big walk. Literally. Only 3.7 miles and 800 feet of descent to the Water Gap to go. We observed our neighbors, the bikini girl and hippie, occupying a single sleeping bag for two. We were visited too by the unmistakable scent of a certain psychoactive plant burning its way in our direction from nearby campsites. But as prurient as the young-adult activity around us was, we were already deliciously high from our own fun and eager to get back on the trail and finish up. Awaiting us downriver were hot dogs and birch beers from Johnny's on Route 46 and a final lazy summer of child's play before heading into high school.

By the end probably no experience in my early teens proved to be in equal parts as physically challenging and satisfying as this hike. Reviewing it decades later, I think that the expedition marked the conclusion of a childhood of relatively uncorrupted innocence and the start of something less insouciant: adulthood and its inherent complications. Regardless, this fifty-miler (padded if it was) demonstrated to myself that I had what it took to take on the great Appalachian Trail.

9. Camp Brugmann
Adirondack Mountains, New York; 1970

As I was breaking into trail hiking in '69 and '70 in Vermont, on the AT in New Jersey, and still discovering secrets of the woods at Cushetunk Mountain, the Brugmanns were already well versed in putting on boots, packing up supplies, and heading into the wilds. As Jeb told me, his family had a camping tradition centered in upstate New York's magnificent Adirondack Park dating back to his grandparents' generation. Six million acres of forestlands, mountain vistas, and sparkling lakes, too many to count. With roots in the Syracuse area on their dad's side, Bob, Jeb, and their kid brother Paul became natural Adirondackers, exposed to this almost otherworldly place from early childhood.

But for all their grandeur and Olympic fame, the Adirondacks from my experience might be the least broadly known group of mountains in the northeastern U.S., a less familiar destination than the New Hampshire Whites, Catskills, or even the Poconos. People I come across today who live a day's drive south from these beauties—friends and neighbors, high school classmates, etc.—are either magnetized by the ADK, go there often, know every detail about every trail and peak, and talk incessantly about them. Or they know little about this forest preserve the size of Vermont beyond a hockey game in Lake Placid in 1980 and prefer to pursue their leisure at more southerly localities. Thus the Adirondacks for many qualify as the most heavenly place on God's earth—or for others as some northern outpost of bogs, bugs, bobsledding, and six months of snow to avoid.

The same summer I did my first AT hike with the Three Bridges troop, Jeb told me the three brothers with their father, W. James Brugmann, undertook their most important Adirondacks adventure. ADK hiking is, in a word, tough. It is step for step the single hardest place I've hiked outside of Maine's epic Katahdin. ADK trail conditions range from rough, marked, and modestly maintained to extremely rough, poorly marked, and effectively unmaintained with the worst of the unmarked trails known as herd paths. All trails, even the better ones, often double as drainage for small streams and spring run-off. Hikes that were rated "easy" really were moderate, and those designated "moderate" were difficult. Anything beyond a moderate rating requires extra caution and time and may not be advisable for the novice. A simple ADK outing can often feel more like going into combat than embarking on a jaunt through the woods. It's imperative that visitors know what they're in for before they head out for a few hours, a day, or overnight.

The Brugmanns set up camp at Colden Lake in the High Peaks Wilderness area and hiked to Algonquin Peak. At 5,114 feet, Algonquin is the second highest of the nearly fifty Adirondack mountains that rise to 4,000 feet or higher and have captured the fancy of the ADK hiking community. According to a friend who has hiked every Adirondack 4,000-footer, participants can get to Algonquin from Colden Lake on a circuitous trail that leads first to Iroquois, which at 4,843 feet is another crusher of a climb. Or one could hike directly to Algonquin on one of the park's notorious herd paths: the Colden Lake-to-Algonquin shortcut with its excessively steep face for which ADK guidebooks advise that hikers, for their safety, stick to ascents only.

After the Brugmanns reached Algonquin via the longer, albeit less intimidating route, they returned in weather that had turned so stormy that the family party lost the trail or elected to return on the shorter but steeper and inadvisable herd path, which was challenging to find and follow. It was here, on the Algonquin descent, the legend of Bob Brugmann was born. For it was he who identified the way and led all down the precipitous route back to the lake, safely and accounted for, including the struggling eleven-year-old Paul. Bobby, 14, saved the day and, as Jeb put it, "showed he had the stuff."

Of course, any discussion of the brothers' early schooling in camping and hiking and their love of the outdoors must also account for the role of scouting. When Bob and Jeb were pre-teen boy scouts, the expectation placed on them was to attend summer camp at Pahaquarra. Located north of the Delaware Water Gap, Pahaquarra sat on a lush thousand acres along the river. Nearby up on the on Kittatinny Ridge stood Mohican, a second large facility that served New Jersey troops into the mid-seventies. Both camps went into decline and shuttered when their properties transferred to the National Park Service in the fallout of the Tocks Island project. But as Jeb confirmed, his and Bob's camp stays included introductory hikes on local Appalachian Trail segments from the Water Gap to Blue Mountain Lakes, some twelve to fifteen miles. Thus their scouting experience and ADK expeditions combined had prepped the two older Brugmann boys for the bigger challenges to come with a readiness quite advanced for a couple of kids just fourteen and twelve.

10. Appalachian Trail, Part II
Delaware Water Gap, Pennsylvania; April 1971

Among the kids back at Readington School who were boy scouts, the anticipation of the Three Bridges' troop's Appalachian Trail fifty would have generated some hallway and homeroom chatter and possibly envy. Our scouts were sixth, seventh, and eighth graders who, as friendly rivals, represented troops lodged in Stanton, Whitehouse, and Readington (the village), as well as George Hill's Three Bridges troop. Bob Brugmann, himself a scout, was no doubt aware of Three Bridges' hiking ambitions. Alas his own troop, the Readington group, was not so active. Due to declining interest and low participation, his scouting experience didn't meet his expectations. Eventually he'd leave the troop and see it fall apart. Therefore, Bob well knew about our pending summer of 1970 High Point-to-Water Gap backpack trip and would be keenly interested in hearing about its joys and hijinks from me and George after we returned to school as HCHS freshmen in the fall.

Early-to-mid adolescence is a period awash in pimples, growth spurts, and personal drama. Entering high school, with our Readington class of 152 swelling to 500, exacerbated this hormonal earthquake by upending the social order we'd formed back at middle school. As freshmen, though confined to our own building, if you didn't share a homeroom, lunch table, bus ride, or class with an old pal, or didn't play on a team or march together in the band, your grade-school connections became subject to lost vitality and breakage. Beginning with football, then later into wrestling and baseball, I dove a bit heedlessly into Central's sports landscape and joined the chorus and newspaper. Teachers and counselors urged us to do just that: "Find activities!" "Get involved!" "Make new friends!" That was how you found your way and stayed visible and viable at big, scary HCHS.

I cannot say how my best buddy from Readington, George, plied these complicated corridors and social waters. But I suppose that he didn't have much choice of an extracurricular life. He was needed at home to help his elderly pop keep the declining Three Bridges store going. One way or another, we managed to carry over the middle school friendship into early high school. During Easter break I jumped into a second Appalachian Trail hike with George and his gritty scout troop.

Our spring '71 expedition was a short but important extension of our 1970 High Point-to-Water Gap hike with a lean crew of seven led by a seventeen-year-old Eagle scout, Will Burgh. Under Will's direction, the walk condensed into three days of eleven to seventeen miles and, importantly, reached the Pennsylvania side of the Delaware Water Gap, forty-two miles. My one distinct memory of the trip, however, is a bit weird.

All had started out fine despite it being mid-April and cold at night with patches of snow lingering on the ridgetop. Around lunchtime the second day, Troop 186 emerged from the woods into a tumult of uprooted trees and bulldozers, which I recorded in my notes as Lake Success. In this mayhem we had entered, Will lost the white AT blazes and for twenty or thirty minutes we found ourselves stuck in this noisy, dusty confusion, unsure of where to escape.

The area we were hiking through, known by the real estate moniker Blue Mountain Lakes, was in a fury of transition. Starting in 1956, hundreds of second homes perched above a chain of small manmade lakes had been built here and connected by new roads. Without today's federal protections, walking the Appalachian Trail half a century ago more than occasionally meant bumping into places like this and having to pivot around new development. And, well, this was New Joisey, boys. What could we expect, just miles and miles of woods?

It was in the late sixties when this funny thing happened to folks on their way to the BML vacation cottages: the U.S. government swooped in and purchased the mountain and valley for the massive Tocks Island Reservoir. The government then kicked everybody out and condemned every home, farm, and village. And, as if to add insult to injury, the planned thirty-seven-mile-long flood-control impoundment of the Delaware River was scrubbed; defeated by some of the same enviro crowd that rallied to save Sunfish Pond. The government kept the 70,000 acres taken for the project and created one of America's most accidental parks, the Delaware Water Gap National Recreation Area.

I remembered the dirt, the machinery, the chaos. What I couldn't say with full confidence is whether this was the end of the beginning, a final burst of new homes, or the beginning of the end: the government-ordered removal of these family hideaways. Memory impulses tell me what we encountered was new construction, though an article in *Skylands Visitor* magazine on the development specified 1969 as the final year of building in the area. I may never know for sure.[4]

Eventually, we found the continuation of the white AT blazes and the hike proceeded. Next day, instead of ending on the familiar Jersey side of the Water Gap as we had the summer before, Will's trek crossed the toll bridge and nominally penetrated Penn's Woods to a campsite at the Council Rock overlook above the Delaware River.

Will's push over the river was perhaps my inspiration to heed Horace Greeley's clarion call to "Go West, Young Man" and leave New Jersey, as entering Pennsy introduced me to a new AT state with untapped possibilities for later adventure. Indeed, it was to PA where Bob Brugmann and I would go when we stepped on the trail together soon after for the first time.

---

[4] I returned to Lake Success to look around in 2020. Few traces of the second-home community remain, and the NPS maintains the old roads as foot and bike trails. Exploring the area and imagining how it appeared sixty years ago is fun. With buildings gone, the land has healed and the forest grown back. You can circle four or five remnant lakes on gentle trails without the bustle of human activity from the past. For more reading, see "Paradise Lost, and Found" at www.njskylands.com.

Part Two
School Daze

11. America's Game
Flemington; 1970-71

"Brugmann?... Where's Bobby Brugmann, dammit?... Brugmann!"

I could still hear gravel-throated Stan Dreswick calling for my buddy—a fellow second-stringer—for a surprise game entry. Why I remembered Bob's summons from old Mr. Dreswick, the assistant coach, I can't exactly say. Hmm. If Brugmann is called, get ready; I could be next. If he gets to play, why not me? Did my friend's opportunity ahead of mine ruffle some feathers, hence the enduring ego bruise?

For a pair of boys with medium builds and not much in the way of muscles or a nasty streak, freshman football was probably an unwise choice. But how were Bob and I to know? At HCHS you found your way into respectability and popularity via sports, band, or the performing arts. Short of that, the poor soul adrift faced the prospect of four years of swimming for the pool safety ladder and just as often smacking into its concrete walls.

Football thus was a tempting choice for any sports-inclined ninth-grade kid with a few grams of grit and scoops of guts gathered from neighborhood pigskin skirmishes in Whitehouse Station, Ringoes, or Raritan Gardens. So Bob and I passed our physicals, reported for practice on September 1, and hung on as Red Devils for one unremarkable season. With his advantages in speed and bulk, Brugmann trained as a back, now classified in football parlance as a "skill" position. At 143 lbs., I was a designee linebacker, assigned to that hybrid defensive role because I had no identifiable talent other than a propensity to pile on others. Mostly, we occupied two seats on Coach Wright's bench. Over the seven games Bob would tally seven yards of rushing offense. I made cameos in a few routs. We had no future in football.

But quitting anything we started, such as a hike, a pet project, a volunteer activity, went against our respective natures. So sophomore year Bob and I jumped in for a second go without much thought. However, after a week of holding plastic body bags, a.k.a. tackling dummies, for varsity players to smash into and growl, I saw the handwriting on the wall and turned in my helmet, pads, and cleats. With the junk they issued us scrubs, I was a live target for a shattered bone or blow to the kidney and knew it. Ahead of a trip up Route 31 to the hospital emergency room, I got out.

The ever-braver Brugmann lasted longer. In fact, he stuck with football long enough to appear in the JV team photo in the program book sold at the stadium; long enough to know he wasn't going to get playing time. As he was one never to waste precious hours kissing the butt of a coach or any authority figure, Bob too would relent and give up the dream of gridiron glory before September was out.

We had our flings with America's Game and saw we didn't belong. Besides getting beat on by a bunch of brawlers for scant opportunities to show our stuff, the locker room culture at HCHS was a poor fit for independent thinkers like us. When we got dumped into the same practice environment with the varsity, it was awful. Our dressing space was a cesspool of bullying, racism, misogyny, homophobia, and hostility towards scholastic achievement. If you were on the team, smart, and dedicated to studies, it was best to hide it and play dumb. I didn't stick around long enough to be hazed in this setting. But had I, my manliness surely would have been tested in uncomfortable ways. These were the times in which we lived.

There was, however, a silver lining to our departures. Quitting football, it turned out, set the stage for an expansion of our friendship and shift in the direction of our lives—to the Appalachian Trail. Bob and I had logged one hike on the trail the past spring to Pennsylvania. Now that we were unshackled from going to practices, we set our sights on more trips. Instead of languishing as benchwarmers or collateral for the better athletes to demonstrate their value to the coaches, Brugmann and I would team up to blaze new trails and find adventure in a style of our own, far from the drudge of the daily bus rides and every other kind of high school crap. These journeys into the wilds of the East would profoundly stir our souls. They continue to stir mine today.

12. Westward Ho
Wind Gap, Pennsylvania; May 1971

Our bonding that began in freshman football rose to new heights when Bob and I, along with a promising newcomer, hit the Appalachian Trail at Mount Minsi as the ninth-grade year wound down. By now I had two AT backpacking trips on my resume while Bob, still consigned to the juvenile standards of his scout troop, burned for a piece of this higher-end trail action. What the scoutmasters and troop kids couldn't deliver to Brugmann, an honest fanny-busting adventure, hiking with me might accomplish. Getting into the woods was also a way for us to cope with the chillier realities of HCHS, where my friend and I found ourselves more and more on the outside of the main channels to popularity: gridiron stardom, band, basketball, baseball, wrestling, stage, or dating a cheer squad or color guard girl. Screw all that. We'll walk the Appalachian Trail!

   The newbie guarding the rear was none other than Bob's up and coming kid brother by nineteen months, Jeb. Just a slender eighth-grade band lad, the boy was also a fast learner. In no time Jeb would ascend to Appalachian Trail wunderkind.

Eager to expand our reach on the famous pathway beyond the familiar been-there-done-that ridgeline of northwest New Jersey, our troika struck into Pennsy from the Water Gap and progressed as far as Wind Gap, a respectable 15.5 miles, and set up a campsite. Then overnight a nor'easter swept in, overpowered our tent, clothing, and packs and continued to dump rain into the next morning. Uncharacteristic of us, we gave into our shared misery. At a phone booth in town, Bob called Millie, who rescued us a couple of hours later in her Jeep Wagoneer. Our planned second day of fifteen additional miles to Little Gap was wiped out due to waterlogged boots, wet cargo, and three dampened, partly broken spirits.

On the day ahead of the monsoon, the skies were sunny, and we were clipping along. The mercury broke 80 F, the views were good, and for each mile we advanced into PA, we felt a welcome disconnect from our Jersey breeding and its provincialism. Bye, bye to Flemington, HCHS, and Del Water Gap. Hello to endless chain of mountains leading to—that's right—frickin' Georgia!

But as any experienced AT hiker will attest, the trail in the Keystone State is a rather monotonous ridgetop slog bedeviled with pile after pile of jagged rocks, therefore known by many foot travelers as "Rocksylvania." Though a mere youngster, Jeb negotiated each cleave or crack we encountered with the polish of a seasoned trekker. Together, the Brugmanns worked as a well-oiled tandem irrespective of task. Even at this age, Bob and Jeb were adept at gathering kindling for the fire, setting up the tent, breaking it down, or folding up their sleeping bags with precision before tying them to their pack frames. Like a pair of prancing wildcats you might observe at a zoo, the brothers made ascents or descents on tricky slopes and slides look seamless and natural. While I came to expect this much from Bob, I marveled that Jeb was as capable in both the physical and technical affairs of backpacking as his older sibling.

To be fair, I had the fortitude—the sheer determination—to keep up with the Brugmanns' brisk pace for any long day's haul. But around the campsite and in other "skill" aspects of outdoor living, not so much. Compared to this scout-trained brotherhood, I was strictly an understudy; a willing spirit but also a bungler. Bob and Jeb knew what they were doing. I faked my way through the unfamiliar, sucked in some pride, and accepted any helping hands either brother might graciously offer. Which being mature beyond their age, they did patiently and graciously.

One strange occurrence from this trip begs telling. Trailside camping is permitted mostly everywhere along the AT, and we selected a spot in some woods a quarter mile from Route 115 (today's PA 33) to pitch our tent. Though we were close enough to hear highway noise, we couldn't see the roadway. The site was also a few hundred yards from our drinking-water source: a mountain stream tucked deeper in the woods. The next morning, as Bob and Jeb fought the storm to tear down our camp and pack up, I sauntered off to the stream to wash breakfast plates and utensils and refill canteens.

It's important to note that I had a sharp sense of direction. My brain ordinarily functioned like the fluid merger of a topographical map, GPS, and compass. I was also in my element happy in the woods. Out here felt safe. To fixate on the unlikely possibility of any variety of mishap seemed to me a waste of energy and source of needless anxiety. I didn't obsess about bear attacks or breaking my ankle from a fall. Rather, I soaked in the beauty and welcomed respite from life's less enjoyable complications away from the trail.

But the ongoing rain that morning had followed a long night of leaky-tent distress. And walking back from the stream, I lost my way. Apparently from the combination of the rain and a thick, low cloud deck, the din from the highway dispersed in such a way as to create a kind of echo chamber. My normally pinpoint spatial instincts were thrown into confusion.

I called out for Bob and Jeb, but there was no response save for rain patter and the road noise that continued to bounce pell-mell from indeterminate directions. For a walking, breathing road atlas like me to be this directionally turned around, even for a matter of minutes, was very uncomfortable. Thankfully, the brothers soon enough heard my pleas for help and rescued me. Rattled but unharmed, I made my way back to camp. End of incident. And yet...

There are stories about adventurers who wander off from shelter in blizzards and die. Illogically or not, the idea that 200 yards from safety I might amble off and succumb to hypothermia entered my active fourteen-year-old imagination. Although what happened on Blue Mountain that morning was not life threatening and, even without the brothers' verbal rejoinder, it would've resolved itself, as it did. Still, it freaked me out. I loved the woods. The further from cars, trucks, and people, the better. But to be inside an unfamiliar forest, drenched, chilled, not knowing which way was the way out, this was a circumstance outside my comfort zone.

In hiking, bad things occur when one would least expect it. Injuries and accidents were rare on precipitous and slippery slopes. Rather they begin with a trip on an unseen tree root that would send someone flailing like a hockey goalie in pursuit of an unlikely save. And from the source incident, any ensuing wandering off, getting lost, or panic—all which seized me that soggy morning—could escalate into something far worse than the relative innocuousness of the original mishap.

Hazards lurk when humans and nature under stress find

themselves, unbeknownst, on a collision course.

In an air of mild disappointment, Bob, Jeb, and I made peace with our decision to bail. Packs hoisted, we trudged a mile into Wind Gap in squishy boots and splurged on a hot meal at Bonser's while waiting for Millie. We must've been a puzzling sight for the locals at the café's counter: three kids off the Appalachian Trail, dripping wet, with no adult. The absurdity of us sitting in Bonser's would become part of Brugmann/Lobb trail lore and keep us three laughing during my next two years of hiking with the brothers. If only all such encounters with nature could so humorously end.

13. Sophomore Slide
Flemington; 1971-72

Once elevated to sophomore year, Bob and I, along with nearly five-hundred other victims of our circumstances entered a physical space that was about as cheerful as an institution for the sick. As freshmen we'd tasted the good life in the splendor of HCHS's newly opened Lower House where we sampled the nectars of the big expansion while ensconced inside a safe haven, miles away it felt from the original factory-inspired, smokestack-decked Upper House complex.

Shifting to the Upper House with its tight hallways and dingy stairwells felt more like a demotion than the intended grade promotion. The Sophomore Wing of the Upper House was one long banal corridor. Its classroom views took in Central's gunky practice football field and parking for the school's fleet of yellow buses. Every morning at 10:30, a revolting mix of boiled hot dogs, French fries, and waxed bean odors would escape the cafeteria and waft its way into our space. Despite having a semi-exclusive section of the school to our own, we were regularly raided by older, hyper-hormonal upperclassmen with cars and dubious motives who'd slip in to check out our girls and work them over with their slick lines and promised rubber-wheeled adventures.

Thus if you were a HCHS sophomore, a couple of regular guys like Brugmann or I who did not have a team, musical group, popular girlfriend, or a part in that year's school musical, *The Sound of Music*, to shape an identity, social extinction was a palpable threat.

I muddled through the year by writing a few pieces for the school paper, *The Lamp*, and found an anchorage with some of Central's cool kids in Interact, a service club headed by Ken Lobb, a senior at this time. Indeed, my ex-tormentor brother, by forcing me into leadership roles in the club, saved my shaky sophomore ass from death by anonymity.

What exactly Bob was doing then eluded me, though I had a recollection of his contributing to student government causes and dipping into school and community activism. Motivated by late-sixties' anti-Vietnam venom, the classes ahead of ours raised enough newsworthy hell to make the local papers. Central's protesters, however, weren't limited to the usual fringe radicals. Rather our rebellious ranks were comprised of brainy council types, organization presidents, and letter-sweater-wearing captains pulled mainly from the Flemington-Raritan population, which included the affluent kids residing in some of the township's woodsiest enclaves. We also had a cohort of shaggy-haired, peacenik-type teachers. Whether or not you were at ease with its political atmosphere, or found safety in the school's complex social network, the early seventies proved to be a fascinating time at Central.

The year Bob and I entered high school, in 1970, was likely the peak of student activism at Central. From '72 and after, with the military draft slowing down and the eighteen-year-old vote secured, activism's sharpest edges would soften in fervor and tone. When our class graduated and moved on to college in '74, the campus life we found enjoyed every advantage of the era with little threat of disruptions from unruly protests. Things had quieted down appreciably.

But before that all happened, Bob found a calling in Central's waning embers of activism: environmental, student-rights, personal freedoms, and peace activism. It was at an assembly in the auditorium, sophomore year, when I first witnessed Brugmann's stunning refusal to recite the Pledge of Allegiance. Bob and other objectors around the school had done their homework and determined that standing for the Pledge was required of citizens under law; but speaking it or placing the right hand over your heart was not. Though he respectfully stood during the morning recitation, he did so silently. Despite some initial backlash towards the protesters, the administration ultimately chose to forgo disciplining them. Before long, participation in the ritual, full or partial, was left to the individual.

To be sure, I wasn't clear as to what Bob was objecting. Was it the "Under God" part? Or the larger, overarching principle of declaring a personal obedience to a flag that represented a government with a military-industrial complex that continued to send boys not much older than us to the jungles of Southeast Asia to die in a war that for many felt senseless?

Back then I was living in a Republican home with a proud father who served in World War II and flew the Stars and Stripes outside the house every Memorial Day, Vets Day, and Fourth of July. My college-educated mother, though not as conservative, would tow the party line until the turn of the new century when she no longer trusted GOP positions on much of anything and cast a vote for the morally ambidextrous Bill Clinton himself. At fifteen I didn't know how to react to Bob as his activism and advocacy continued to mature. At that time my limited political awareness tended to seesaw from Dad's staunch opposition to Democrats and war protesters to Ken's embrace of youth culture and the struggles of minorities.[5]

So Bob's powerful, and very public, political stance in 1971 was confusing for me. I didn't know how to take it. I didn't know how it fit—or didn't—into the fabric of our friendship. After all, Dad had long advised me against associating with "those damn hippies." Perhaps that was what was happening to Brugmann: with his lengthening hair and leftist ways of thinking, he was transitioning to one. Yet, despite any space our differing levels of interest in the politics of the day might have created between us, we continued to nurture a friendship that went beyond hiking.

By turns we'd laugh and groan about the stupid people and policies we encountered daily at Central. But, as with so many of the things we'd experienced together in the two years since Readington School, Bob was steps, if not leaps and bounds, ahead of me, in such areas as his grades, his future, his camping and backpacking proficiency. Even at work, Bob made himself a star dishwasher. Now he led the way in politics too, setting a standard that challenged me in ways which life to this point had simply not prepared me to handle.

One thing in which we were equals was our struggles with girls. As I saw it, girls worth the effort of taking out dated "up" with older boys with cars, or even college guys. Thus a kid without a vehicle could expect no date. As we were now floating untethered from sports and the school's other social epicenters, Bob and I faced the Monday-to-Friday grind a little lost in cliquish hallways without the comforts of a cuddly companion. Bob and Cherie Nordstrom had faded into history, and neither he nor I possessed the chutzpa one

---

5   My political lassitude ended with Al Gore's loss to George W. Bush in the 2000 election.

needed to break through with any other choice classmate.

Instead of dwelling on what we didn't or couldn't have, we turned to planning hikes. During free periods we'd head to the library, unroll topo maps, study guidebooks, and plot and dream about long walks in the woods away from Central's stinkpot of rules, immature peer behavior, and girls who paid us no attention. We hit the Appalachian Trail three times sophomore year.

14. Steppingstones to Georgia
Lehigh Gap, Pennsylvania; October 1971

In the weeks between our quitting football and Columbus Day, Brugmann and I planned a humdinger of a hike. The two of us, with the freshman phenom Jeb again on board, would strike deeper into Pennsylvania, from Wind Gap westward to a highway crossing known as Blue Mountain Summit: thirty-six miles of mainly level but unrelentingly rocky trail. We'd cover twenty-two miles the first day, including the famously vertiginous descent into Lehigh Gap, camp in a shelter, and finish with an easier fourteen the next. Bob and I were fifteen, Jeb newly fourteen. What on earth were we thinking?

The 22.2 miles of AT we walked that warm Saturday remains my third-longest single-day lifetime hike. From what we gathered from the new *Backpacker* magazines we scoured in the HCHS library, the twenty-mile trail day was standard fare for any worthy long-distance hiker. Of course, I nailed nineteen in a day on my first AT outing sixteen months before in New Jersey. What was to stop us from doing a little extra now?

He Was Too Young To Die

More recently, without the benefit of the flexibility of my youth, I've hiked the Appalachian Trail's notorious Lehigh Gap descent and ascent and not found it to be exceptionally intimidating. It required rock scrambling, two or three short fanny rolls, and was mildly exposed; but not as nerve-inducing as say the Chin on Mount Mansfield. In the dry weather, Bob, Jeb, and I did our descent into the gap comfortably enough. However, when you load thirty-five pounds on your backs and add twenty miles of leg fatigue near the end of a very long trail day, the precipitous drop was for us youngsters, with our limited experience, an important physical and psychological victory.

What happened next turned out to be a bigger issue than that earlier bit of bouldering. First suggestion of trouble was a parking lot full of wide, sagging vans where we re-entered the woods from across the gap. *Could it be, please not be, BSA?* Minutes later, now approaching our anticipated accommodations with reserves of daylight and stamina low, we feared the telltale signs of a full shelter: food and firewood smells, the World Series crackling on a portable radio, and a dozen excited, adolescent voices bouncing through the trees. Scouts indeed had hiked from the vans and covered the shelter environs with their tarps, sleeping bags, and camping whatnot. We were screwed.

The troopers' occupation of the Outerbridge Shelter forced Bob, Jeb, and I in our weariness to lug ourselves uphill another fifteen minutes to find ground level enough to raise a tent; never mind the long walk back to our water source near the shelter. Later, in darkness, we managed to boil up some dried mac-and-cheese as the hootenanny continued below us. *Damn the lazy shits!* What could we do other than laugh, curse, and try to sleep.

Next morning, we shrugged off the effects of the previous evening and resumed loving life on the AT. Along the ridgeline we passed the New Jersey Zinc smelting works at Palmerton. Back in those days it was in full production. A site of industrial might to marvel, if one overlooked its morbid, vegetation-poisoning pollution. Farther along, more to our liking, we soaked in the thirty-mile view from Bake Oven Knob and enjoyed a vigorous scramble up Bear Rocks.

I suspected it was atop these rocks, with their nice view of the Poconos, that Bob and Jeb would first muse upon the mystical Maine-to-Georgia hike. And later in their mother's car on the drive back to New Jersey, share their dream with Millie. If we could endure everything the weekend had thrown us—major rock scrambles, punishing long days, improvised camping—how bad could a thru-hike be? But if this idea had infected the brothers, it didn't me. Two days and a night was pushing my adventure limits. As much as I liked to hike, my preference was to recuperate from a day's work with a shower and fluffy pillow than any of the myriad tasks and discomforts that accompany extended backpacking. In almost any test of trail toughness, I was no match for these two.

15. Growing Pains
Flemington; 1971-72

It's tough, maybe impossible, to pinpoint when and how teenage male friendships evolve from casual buddy stuff into something deeper. Did Bob and I discuss sensitivities, emotions, what we felt inside our hearts and heads? No, of course not—you can't converse about what you barely understand. Certainly, we had a substantial overlap in interests and enough shared experience and compatibility to develop the strong connection we did. But was it solid and even nimble enough to endure Bob's turn toward leftist politics, his intense focus on the environment, or my unsatisfied social impulses? And there were my sloppy backpacking skills to consider; quite inferior in comparison to his.

By mid-freshman year, Bob and Cherie Nordstrom amicably called off their romance, or consented to turn down the temperature to strictly a friends level. I remember receiving this news on a hike. Without saying much, I could sense that Bob was disappointed, if not aggrieved. Despite the odds against it working, Bob and Cherie had apparently agreed to allow each other to date others at school, believing they could rise above the jealousies that often ensue when a former love interest directs their attentions to a competing paramour. I can't recall the specifics of what separated them, but as is the case with many young couples throughout the ages, Bob and Cherie flourished for a period, hit the inevitable bumps, snags, and obstacles along the way, then fizzled.

Without knowing their interpersonal dynamics, the two looked the part of a well-matched pair. They were bright, affable, very active in school, good-looking and goal-oriented teens. Although Cherie was already following her creative instincts into the performing arts, she and Bob shared interests in student government and policy and the progressive politics of the day: eighteen-year-old voting rights, American troop withdrawals from Southeast Asia, equal rights, and Gloria Steinem-era feminism.

Where I suspect that they encountered headwinds was in how each prioritized finding their place within Central's tricky social landscape. Once Bob dropped football, he punted away his best opportunity for a normal high school experience centered in friends and frivolity. Instead, he turned inward and became laser-focused on hiking and environmental activism all the while keeping his grades at least ballpark competitive with the strongest scholastic achievers in the class.

In Bob's view the school routine by sophomore year had become little more than a supervised playground of cliques and rules, anchored by an uninspired curriculum taught by coasting tenured teachers there for the paycheck and union benefits to students being warehoused before they move on to college and got started in earnest on a purposeful career track. There were very notable exceptions to this perception, but being kids, Bob, our peers, and I tended to pick on our less dynamic faculty rather than give due credit to the top performers in their ranks.

Thus HCHS had become, for my friend, a mildly annoying and intellectually under nourishing waystation to wade through until he graduated. But any nitpicking about the education quality aside, with his brains, maturity, and focus, grounded in boy-scout common sense, Bob might have selected any of a dozen career paths and risen high in the pursuit of his choice. Some directions he might have taken had he made it to college and beyond include law, government, policy, political office, forest ecology, climate science, land conservation, social or environmental activism, sustainability, teaching, or journalism. The possibilities were manifold and, for Bob, all attainable.

What about architect, his declared ambition in the eighth-grade yearbook? Not as likely, unless he specialized in the design of what we'd come to know as green buildings.

When I consider our generation's top environmental figures, people in the league of Vice President Al Gore, the writer Bill McKibben, or veteran climate scientist James Hansen, I can't shake the thought of how Bob Brugmann might have fit in at this level of influence had he circumvented the accident and landed a career in an area of environmental protection. As a high-ranking official in President Gore's administration, could Bob, Al, and others have energized our country's foot-dragging response to global warming three decades ago and put the U.S. in a world leadership position more unified to fight and save a threatened planet?[6]

Had he not perished so young, Bob might have changed the world. That's how capable of a guy he was.

---

[6] Al Gore's urgent calls to the climate crisis in his 2006 book and documentary film, *An Inconvenient Truth*, today sound both prescient and nostalgic in view of our global emergency, warped politics, and continuing record of wishy-washy environmental action.

By eleventh grade he had only just begun to show the rest of us this prowess in his clarity of thought and totality of commitment to causes. A schoolmate recalled Bob's solid, if unspectacular, class rank of thirty-ninth (top eight percent) at HCHS. My friend probably wasn't going directly to Princeton, but he'd get a good undergrad education somewhere and ascend steadily in his selected area of professional interest. Of that I had no doubt.

Or he might have elected to live off-grid in a cabin on his terms; getting by doing trail or park maintenance to fund the occasional backpacking trip to Alaska, Patagonia, or Mont Blanc. Maybe he'd author books and magazine pieces about his travels as an adventure journalist in the vein of Jon Krakauer. Or been a humble doer who devotes decades of life to managing an environmentally responsible hikers' hostel along the AT. As his mother insisted to me many years after the fall, "Bob would've lived in the woods." Though I didn't dismiss that possibility, I firmly believed that Millie, Jeb, and influential academic mentors would have pushed my friend in a direction where they felt that he could make an impact through his work while also earning a good wage.

In any case, by age fifteen or sixteen my friend could realistically follow any of these avenues. There was nothing foreseeable stopping him.[7]

Cherie, meanwhile, made her mark at HCHS as a dancer, singer, actor, and the class secretary. If Bob had cut himself off from much of the fun that makes high school a rollicking good time before life turns serious, Cherie found a more social passage through Central. She informed me decades later that by sophomore year she'd become romantically interested in a popular guitar-strumming classmate with a

---

7   Jeb lays out his thoughts about what his brother's post-high school life and pathway to a career might have looked like in a later chapter

mellower outlook on life.

While test-score separation at Readington and HCHS effectively confined Cherie and I to different academic and social orbits, by senior year we were both members of Central's track and field team. This by itself was an ambitious step for her as track was a new offering for girls born out of the passage of Title IX. As teammates might have, a few weeks before graduation Cherie and I were drinking at an end of season celebration at another senior's house. Catching me off guard, she approached me and told me, "You're funny when you're drunk." Really? Are you serious? This was almost a year after Bob's death, and one of my rare one-on-ones with Brugmann's classy former good friend. Only later did I figure out she had been flirting with me; and we never became close friends despite our common ties to Bob.

What I've always imagined was in that alcohol-lit moment Cherie saw me as a spinoff Bob with his guard down and sense of humor up. Moreover, while it's useless all these decades later to conjecture whether she and I might have paired up in the wake of the track party, I do lament we never had the opportunity for the riveting, soul-exposing conversation about our mutual friend while the pain of his death was raw. We might have shared privileged stories and secrets because other than Jeb and his mother Millie, who knew Bob as well as Cherie and I did? Nobody, I suspected.

Cherie left the area, got a good education, raised a daughter, married a couple of times, and found a niche as an award-winning auto sales professional in North Carolina. Fifty-two years after she met Bob at Readington School, she and I finally had that face-to-face talk about those years from 1969 to 1973.

16. Personality Spectrum
Flemington; 1971-72

Bob's inward turn, while more evident after his split with Cherie, is not to say he became a withdrawn, morose teenager. That would be misleading. Any changes in his social station at school had more to do with his own changing priorities than any blanket rejection of age normative behavior. As the business of securing individual rights, protecting the environment, and his own hiking ambitions grew to higher levels, the corresponding value of yukking it up with Central's jocks, looking over displays of miniskirts, or befriending our potheads as means to fit in lost its luster.

By fifteen he had outgrown all this nonsense in favor of larger aspirations. Bob never disliked people, but he had no stomach for immaturity and game playing in relationships. And he was disappointed by any mentoring efforts from adults at school and beyond (coaches, scoutmasters, employers) that fell short of his expectations. As Cherie told me, "Bob was very intense about the things he cared about, and never cared if he was popular or not."

He Was Too Young To Die

I well remember Bob's keen wit and easy laugh. But true enough, when immersed in a demanding hike or processing the latest news about ocean pollution from the Jersey Shore—his greatest passion and worry, respectively—my friend was fully absorbed and prone to plunges into the more contemplative hollows of his personality. Who could fault him? The collapse in planet livability is precisely what he anticipated and dreaded. However, the hyper-serious, intensely focused Bob was only one part of him.

His lighter side saw much of the greedy, materialistic, apathetic, and hypocritical reality around us as odious yet laughable. Together we passed many trail and study hall hours in fine humor dissecting the uselessness of the information we were spoon-fed at school, the social stratification at HCHS that disfavored outsiders like us, or the silly detentions they'd impose on students for sneaking out to McDonald's for lunch. Meanwhile, the human health issue stemming from renegade cigarette smoking in the lavatories went unaddressed for much of our time at Central. But thanks to Bob and some friends' close read of the rules for the daily flag-allegiance ritual, the threat of punishment for these objectors was removed.

For sure, a brainy kid like Bob didn't indulge in the usual age-related shenanigans, including drinking and smoking grass. Whether gifted or cursed by his heightened level of maturity, by sixteen Millie's eldest boy possessed the comportment of a Ph.D. closing in on thirty. It was remarkable, really. And Jeb, son number two, was right there with him. Though uncommonly enlightened amongst us adolescents, I never saw the Brugmanns subject to ridicule for their accomplishments or abilities to see through our miniature world at HCHS and respond to it as full-grown adults. They found a nice niche as two rather self-effacing boys who happened to be exceptionally focused, dedicated to a range of causes, and always on top of their schoolwork. Serious, yet widely liked and admired. They were among our rock-solid achievers who would have quietly landed at Duke or Dickinson instead of commuting to Trenton State, piecemealing themselves through community college, or learning a building trade.

The "other" Bob—relaxed, funny, thoughtful, even sweet—would surface at times and places unexpectedly. Terri Clerico, a classmate and pal of Jeb, would read during free periods in Central's courtyard, an oasis of shrubbery and shade walled in by the hallways of the main building. In spring of 1973, a few weeks before the brothers' departures to the Appalachian Trail, the shy and bookish Terri recalled her reverie one day interrupted by the appearance of Bob, who sat at her bench and opened up. "He talked about this great hike and how wonderful it was going to be. Bob was beaming—just so happy. Usually, he was very reserved." Terri's connection with the Brugmanns would grow into a decades-long friendship with Jeb, but as a HCHS sophomore she says she was "intimidated" by both brothers: their maturity, dedication to ideals, and talent for getting things done. Although her world and Bob's world overlapped during his tenure in Terri's church youth fellowship, that moment in the courtyard had stuck—it being the only time she recalled going deeply into conversation with the sagacious older brother and its portentous timing mere weeks ahead of the accident.[8]

Happy interludes aside, Bob had struggled both mentally and physically. He was medicated for migraines that flared during times of overload. One such time was when my

---

8   A Vermont resident, Terri sees Millie on occasion for lunch. "She's told me how happy she is to know that Bob and I had that talk when we did."

friend unwisely tried out for the school's championship-level wrestling team. Jeb would cite his brother's extended bout with depression in the months after an aborted 1972 hike that ended with an infected foot and more medication.

My own friendship with Bob, as it widened sophomore year, would expand beyond planning and doing some amazing hikes. We took the jobs at the restaurant. We went to movies. Bob joined me, Terri, and other local teens in the social activities of the youth fellowship. With Bob securing the approvals and cooperation from the township government, he and I volunteered in Readington's embryonic recycling program. And, though overpowered by bigger kids with better skills, Brugmann and I teamed up on an intramural basketball team at school—the Sophomore Team we called it. Ragtag as we were, we gave it our all and managed to absorb one drubbing after another with a shrug and laughs.

One thing that continued to divide us was academics. We did not share the same classes, but presumably he was enrolled in HCHS's honors courses with other higher achievers who later became doctors, lawyers, bankers, architects, technology gurus, and professors. While I sunk into a sea of unresolvable algebraic equations and geometry proofs, I imagined Brugmann cruising along, doing perfectly respectable pre-college-level work in calculus, physics, or German. As my friend vied for top grades and formed alliances with Central's brainiest, I dogpaddled along with the rest; managing A's in social studies, hanging on to B's in English, but slipping into an unrecoverable abyss in French, science, and math.

17. Farther & Wider
New York and Pennsylvania, Spring 1972

If Bob, Jeb, and I as friends and hiking companions enjoyed a golden era, a time before cracks from disagreements and diverging interests would surface, it would be the six months that spanned our seminal October '71 Lehigh Gap trip through the spring of the following year. On two Appalachian Trail expeditions during this period, we—there's no other way to say it—kicked ass.

If I had to pick an all-time favorite hike with both brothers, it would be our four-day expedition from the New Jersey-New York borderlands to the Bear Mountain Bridge; Easter vacation, sophomore year. From home base in Readington, backpacking out to Pennsylvania as we'd been doing wasn't that big of a deal. The major roads went that direction; and you could be on the AT following the white blazes from the Wind Gap or Water Gap access points in under an hour.

Getting to the trail in New York, seventy-five or eighty miles away, was a greater task. After the trail departs High Point in New Jersey's northwest, the AT straddled the state

He Was Too Young To Die

line with New York for twenty-five miles or so before turning sharply to the northeast into the winsome woods of Sterling Forest and Harriman-Bear Mountain state parks. Combined, these parks offered a 75,000-acre wonderland of nature within sight of Manhattan. For us three wide-eyed Jersey boys, heading into these wilds was to enter a big unknown.

AT hikers after High Point endured a lengthy road walk across two valleys, past dairy farms with threatening canine activity, before returning to a marked footpath at Wawayanda Mountain. Then clear to Bear Mountain the trail brought three days of unrelenting terrain challenges and frequent vistas. It was close enough to suburbia to hear motorboats thrum below in Greenwood Lake, yet inside a mountain kingdom almost magically shut off from metropolitan New York.

In four days of determined walking, from March 31 to April 3, 1972, Bob, Jeb, and I covered a fresh sixty-two miles of the Appalachian Trail, crossing sixteen named mountains. This came with a full range of seasonal-transition weather: from sunny, to rain, to snow, to brisk and bright. Weighted down with bulky packs, we wriggled our lean teenage bodies through the Lemon Squeezer, an aptly named cavern of boulders the route traversed in Harriman. This was our intro to Maine-like hiking—two miles from the New York State Thruway!

Despite a rather pedestrian elevation profile that tops out at 1,400 feet, the trail here was a dipsy-doodle of ups, downs, and technical features, altogether different from the monotonous ridge of Rocksylvania and the Kittatinny's steady fare of gradual rises and drops into gaps. Then, after a last lug up the steep backside of Bear Mountain, victory within our grasp, it all changed.

Here, at the 1,289-foot summit, the AT crashes into the human tidal wave that marks New York. Bear with its 1930s-built stonework lookout tower, museum, and gentle pathway up from the Hudson attracts a stadium-like attendance on a sunny day. No place on the trail, not even Mount Washington, can match these crowds. It's the Mount Fuji of greater NYC. The walk down the mountain can be as congested as a subway station platform at five o'clock, except nobody's hurrying to catch a train. If you're a tired backpacker hauling a load, as we three were, this can be seriously annoying. But to reach the historic suspension bridge at the river, as any worthy AT hiker ought to, you must first—no way to avoid them—pass a zoo, a stagnant lake with paddleboats, a bustling restaurant, and acres of parking lots. Same as one might hustle through Penn Station to catch the train, just lower your head and push on to the bridge as anonymously as is possible.

This journey was the longest of eight hikes I did with Bob and Jeb from '71 to '73. Other occasions saw us gut out lengthier days, survive shakier sleeping conditions, or tackle rougher terrain. My Brugmann finale with Jeb in New Hampshire, August of '73, was epic in itself—except, regrettably, its awesome beauty and vertiginous thrills couldn't be shared with Bob. But the High Point-to-Bear Mountain hike was unmatched for its stumbled-upon, figure-it-out-as-you-go feeling of a Tom-and-Huck adventure. We were two sophomores and a freshman from nowhere New Jersey, on our own away from home, and dove in. Subject to precipitous cliffs, dilapidated shelters, and changeable weather, but treated to sumptuous views, the savory delights of wilderness walking at the edge of the biggest city we knew. Plus a short but memorable journey into the belly of ancient geological derangement—a free trip if one can worm themselves and their pack through to the other side. When Mike and Millie caught up with us in the parking lot, Bob, Jeb, and I shared that universal feeling of humbled satisfaction known to those who cross a distant finish line, but not easy to verbally encapsulate. Leave it at this: We'd come across many mountains from New Jersey and now arrived at the mighty Hudson, the gateway to New England hiking. A-fucking-men!

◊

Late the next month, May of '72, Bob, Jeb, and I hopped on the trail at Route 309, northwest of Allentown, and walked forty-six miles in two days; 23.4 and 22.6 miles, respectively. My longest and second-longest trail hikes ever. We had to be out of our freakin' juvenile minds.

We probably were because the odd thing I remember from this trip is our intrepid trio missing the Pinnacle. Apparently in some mad dog quest to pile on miles late that first day, in dim light we walked past this famous overlook near Hawk Mountain regarded by AT hikers as the signature view on the entire 229-mile route in Pennsylvania. In our defense, the drop-dead lookout was screened by trees and truck-size boulders and positioned a tad off the marked route; it's easier to blow past than one would think. Still, it's the Pinnacle: a must-see forty-mile vista for anybody who hikes in PA. Would a tourist to Yellowstone fail to catch Old Faithful do her eruption? Stupid us, we never got to admire the view from the Pinnacle.

The next day, after a sweaty climb from the Schuylkill River at Port Clinton, you feel the full drag of Rocksylvania. It's a viewless ridgeline hike that follows gravel fire roads across state hunting lands. In the Commonwealth of PA, where I've lived since 1980, the killing of critters large and small for sport is in the natives' bloodline and, sometimes, their religion and politics too. Where the AT enters "game lands" property, even though it's all public domain purchased by the government with help from hunting-license fees, these 1.5-million acres of field and forest exist for animal propagation and, as I suppose they should, hunter use. Hiking and hunting are disparate cultures: one rooted in the meeting of nature on its own terms while the other is driven by the quest for the capture and consumption of God's bounty. Usually hikers and hunters give each other space, nods of acknowledgement, and nobody gets in the way of the other.

Unfortunately during lengthy passages through the game lands, which encompass around two-thirds of the state's AT route, the overall hiking experience tends to sag. Walking here I found akin to making a long drive through our so-called flyover states: maybe not as uniform as you feared, but one time across Kansas is enough. While inside these hunting preserves, the visiting hiker never seems far enough away from gunshots, carcasses, or encounters with large dudes in camouflage who arrive in tank-size pickups. The wise hiker would walk fast, keep alert, and not stop; and remember to wear blaring, fluorescent colors: yellow, orange, red.

If Bob and Jeb felt they needed a readiness test ahead of their big AT hikes in the works and a year away, they got what they bargained for on this two-day romp 'n' stomp. Our days were on par with any veteran thru-hiker norm. Indeed, this kind of mileage was punishing. Yet for those adapted to the jagged footpath and on a mission, twenty miles or longer a day became routine as a shift at work. Add up the miles and after a week or two or six, the states will follow. It's a bruising way to sightsee the eastern mountains, but certain types of adventurers seem to thrive on it.

By the time our Pennsylvania junket wrapped up, successful as it was, life's breezes had picked up in speed and had begun to steer the Brugmanns and I down separate pathways, bringing an end to our trio's halcyon period.

For Bob and Jeb, it was about satisfying their intensifying calling to the Appalachian Trail. In a few weeks hence this enterprising brotherhood would take their road show to places and ambitions never attempted. With plans for '73 taking root, it was time for an 800-mile shakeout to iron out any remaining kinks and erase doubts.

Part Three

Wind Shifts

18. Ten Singing Nuns
Northwestern New Jersey; August 1972

The hiking was fine, but other parts of life could use improvement. So start of junior year I took a gamble. With encouragement from buddies I joined Central's competitive, yet open to all, cross-country team. This decision was driven by my thirst for a more elevated station in school, which at the midpoint of my four years had sunk to its lowest point. All I could claim in my HCHS ledger of accomplishments was a few newspaper stories, some service club activities, and unsuccessful trials in four sports: football, baseball, basketball, and wrestling. Running cross was about all that was left for me to try.

My timing was good. Almost to the day I started, U.S.A.'s Frank Shorter won the gold medal in the marathon at the Munich Olympics and set off a global explosion in running: competitive, recreational, and fitness running. Long-distance running, it turned out, would snare me into its bosom of swelling popularity and award me a taste of the recognition in school I sought. In fact, success in running would change the trajectory of my life for thirty years.

At first my membership on the team wouldn't curb my enthusiasm for hiking or force a rearrangement of priorities to satisfy the new venture's time and energy demands. As such, a few weeks ahead of my XC debut, Bob and I alone repeated an Appalachian Trail classic: New Jersey's Water Gap-to-High Point ridgetop tour. And for the rest of the calendar year, the Brugmanns and I would march along more or less as we had been.

What memory and trail journal entries together couldn't resolve from this time, however, was a pesky "why" question: why I agreed to a repeat hike of this section of trail. Since Bob, Jeb, and I started on the AT fifteen months before, our habit was to go after new mileage and new vistas in fresh locations with each hike. Unlike me, with those Jersey hikes in '70 and '71 with the Three Bridges scouts, had Bob yet to trample this in-state portion of the AT? Or due to our limited budgets, shift assignments at the restaurant, or some incipient pressure I now felt to not miss training runs for the approaching XC season, were three days up the venerable Kittatinny spine our only workable option for a summer of '72 backpack?

What seemed likely to have driven the decision to hike in New Jersey was simply Bob's desire to fill an AT mileage gap ahead of his 1973 end-to-end journey. It's logical to think he wanted this stretch done, checked off, added to our previous conquests, to earn himself a break in the middle of next summer's projected 2,000-mile trek. His bagging of this mileage would eliminate any need next year to hike the 200-odd contiguous miles from Bear Mountain, New York, across the northwest Garden State, and into Pennsylvania we'd together covered on past trips.

Add to this logic the *illogic* of our on-trail encounter with Jeb. As Bob and I worked northbound towards High Point on day two, Jeb and a friend were walking south near

Culvers Gap. Did Jeb too hope to knock out this piece of our state in advance of his own summer of '73 big AT hike? But more puzzling is the question of why the Brugmanns, *who always hiked together*, were now hiking separately in opposite directions when their objectives it appeared were the same. My best guess was a transportation complication.

To start our hike, Bob and I hitchhiked to the Water Gap, about thirty-five miles from home. From High Point at the conclusion of our expedition, seventy-five miles away, we'd thumb back to Readington. Jeb, in reverse, did the same: hitch to High Point, walk south to the Water Gap. Hitch back from there.

While this method of getting around was not uncommon for youths with backpacks, the odds of grabbing rides were mathematically favorable if two hitched. The chances that some charitable driver would stop to help a couple of kids with no money for a bus were pretty good. But three loaded down with packs and bedroll? The percentages would plunge. With this logic it made sense for each brother, with his own trail buddy, to split up.

While our passage with the younger brother contained a whiff of surprise and seemed collegial enough, the event wasn't staged for fun. Bob and Jeb were assiduous planners, but after conferring with Jeb in 2021, I learned this mid-hike encounter was not pre-scripted from home in the usual family spirit of collaboration. Bob and Jeb, believed to have an unbreakable bond, were apparently at odds. "I got the feeling Bob didn't want me along," Jeb told me. "So I made my own plans."

More intriguing was that the brothers next year would plot actual opposite-direction Appalachian Trail journeys. Bob would begin at Katahdin in Maine, the northern terminus, and hike south. Jeb would start in Georgia and walk north. Had things worked out, the teen adventurers would pass near the trail midpoint in southern Pennsylvania, give or take fifty miles, doing things their own way, on their own schedules, without ill feelings. That was their vision.

Another interesting footnote regarding this backpacking trip was that we conducted our minivacation to the New Jersey mountains with no parental involvement. At ages sixteen (Bob and I) and fourteen (Jeb), we pulled off the full work sans assistance. Other than consent to go, we didn't think we needed adult involvement, nor did we encourage it. After all, fuel emissions from superfluous auto use went against our environmental ethic. Improbable as this way of thinking might stack up with the modern-day expectation of full parental oversight of their teens, in 1972 this was how we thought about and managed our affairs. We walked the walk. Completely and literally.

By the August of '72 hike, our fifth backpacking outing in sixteen months, three days on the trail with Bob had acquired a rhythm. Without talking much we understood our strengths and hiking styles and worked in sync as teammates on daily missions that covered eight, twenty-one, and eleven miles, respectively. All in a day's sweat and toil.

With tenting no longer permitted, we stopped at Sunfish Pond to swim, then pushed on to Rattlesnake Spring to camp. The next night, instead of cramming into a shelter with other hikers, we advanced to the summit of Sunrise Mountain to bed under the summer constellations. For good or bad, this magnificent location has a road to the rest of New Jersey, and our solitude was terminated the next morning before dawn by the arrival of ten singing nuns! In English, Latin, or French verse, I cannot say.

I wasn't much for formal religion beyond the decidedly secular church youth fellowship, but must ask: Where were these cloaked women of mercy eleven months later when Bob reached a critical moment in his big hike and desperately needed higher intervention? Had they been in his midst, then, at that juncture, it's possible this excruciating tale about my friend's misfortune might never need be told.

19. Beast of Beauty & Burden
Georgia to Maine

By the spring of 1972, Bob and Jeb were fixated on the idea of hiking the entirety of the Appalachian Trail. Me? I couldn't picture being out there for more than a week before the toll of the twenty-mile days, lousy food, and bad sleeping conditions would break me down to the point of quitting. Besides, I had now begun a slow, inexorable migration from hiking to running.

Most anyone who invests a significant amount of time on the AT would idealize walking the full distance from Springer Mountain, Georgia, to Maine's Baxter Peak. I imagined it on my first two High Point-to-Water Gap hikes with the boy scouts, and again while backpacking with the Brugmanns. By age sixteen, I had eliminated any serious thought about undertaking an AT "thru-hike."

Why? I was a durable and determined hiker. Fifteen to eighteen-mile days on a repeating cycle were within my range; and in good weather I loved it all. But when it came to overnighting out there, in tent or shelter, I was a lightweight. I didn't care for it then and I don't now.

My early trips with the scouts involved multiple nights of sleeping-bag torment on wooden platforms in open-faced shelters or in tents with nothing but a tarp and feathers to cushion my bones from the damp ground. In these normal circumstances by the rustic standards of the trail, I might snatch a few hours of fitful sleep. But more than any pleasure gleaned from these cowboy-style sleepovers, I fought the elements and, frequently, I lost. Elements such as, but not limited to: buzzing mosquitoes, frigid temperatures, the rutchy, snoring, farting kid next to me, nature's call in the middle of a dark night, or gathering enough elusive comfort to drift off on a hard surface with a pillow improvised from dirty socks and underwear stuffed into the sack that by day encased my bedroll. When it rained, as it did so forcefully that stormy morning in Wind Gap in '71, there were no means of escape. Sooner or later water will find a way inside the tent, wet the bedding, the boots, and penetrate one's pack too. Before breaking camp and moving again, any last vestige of good humor had evaporated.

Ah, and what about food? The sustenance to keep you going and going? Well, a trail lunch back then meant any form of fast, chewy, gooey, salty, crunchy snack: peanuts, candy bars, pieces of fruit, and a scoopful of dried fruits, nuts, and sodium known to hikers as Gorp.™[9] Come evening we'd mix some powdery substance we'd packed, stir it in boiling water, and call it dinner. Food was our greatest source of pleasure or pain on any extended backpack. Mostly, what we had to eat was not nearly enough.

What was clear by junior year was that unlike Bob or Jeb, I was not thru-hiker material. Two or three nights of this, uh, *lifestyle*, and I was craving any moldy campground

---

[9] Today's Whole Foods-fortified and REI-supplied trekkers have ascended to ever-funkier bars and tubes of squeezable syrups for quick oral ingestion and a promised energy rush. Their advertised taste satisfaction and nutritional values are endlessly scrutinized.

pull-cord shower we might sneak into, a roadside stand chocolate shake, Mom's fresh sheets, freedom from bugs, and a real pillow. Time to put me on a bus for home!

As I was familiar with both long runs and long hikes, my tendency was to judge (if imperfectly) the weeks of hardship of an AT super hike against the numbing if short-lived pain of a marathon. More to the point, the urge a hiker feels to take on the trail in full I find analogous to a runner's "itch" to "go the distance" and try a marathon. For the runner, once they finished some 10k or half-marathon events, they might logically think of a marathon as their next, and ultimate, goal. Similarly, if the eager hiker can maintain fifteen, eighteen, or twenty miles a day for a week and put up with many rigors, inconveniences, and depravations that accompany trailside camping (what, no showers, no toilet paper, no cell coverage?), what's to deter them from attempting to walk the entire distance?

One difference between a single-day 26.2-mile run and a four-to-six-month adventure hike is that there are acceptable mitigation strategies to finagle one's way through a marathon and still go home feeling worthy of the medal all who finish get. For instance, one may—as many participants do—run slowly, ponderously, shuffle-like slowly. They may also fast-walk parts of the race and pretend it's running so long as you reach the end within a generous time limit. With staying power, a runner can half-ass-it and still make it to the end.[10]

An AT thru-hike, though, is quite a different animal. To make a thru-hike hurt less, one may cut it up and walk it in manageable-sized pieces, or sections, take days off, shower

---

[10] The aura of the lonely distance runner passed into legend decades ago. Today's marathon is a long-slog social event run in gym shorts or spandex, with entertainment, cheering spectators, and plenty of food and drink stations. It will hurt before it ends. But a high percentage of those who start will finish.

and sleep in off-trail motels, or hire drivers to haul your load—a tactic known as slackpacking. But no legit hiker can cheat on the distance, skip climbs, or lollygag and get to Maine. The more time frittered away in cozy lodgings with good pizza and IPAs, the longer this already unbearably long trip will take.

For Bob Brugmann and his thru-hike vision, it remained unclear when he decided he wanted to walk all the way and committed to the journey. I had assumed he had this epiphany by our second expedition, the October of '71 two-day Lehigh Gap extravaganza. If he and Jeb could come out of a weekend that arduous with nothing worse than banged up toenails and head-to-foot dust, imagine the possibilities for pain, dirt, and dishevelment over the span of a months-long fourteen-state enterprise! Also around this time, a trail enthusiast from Virginia, Edward Garvey, came out with a book that Bob and Jeb devoured that told of Garvey's then-novel thru-hike experience.

To be clear, Bob wasn't alone in formulating a plan to fulfill this dream. Jeb's involvement should not be overlooked or seen as less important. As Jeb would later reveal, Bob's enthusiasm for thru-hiking would flag at times while brother number two kept the fires burning. As the older sibling by nineteen months, Bob earned respect as the family sage. But it was both Brugmann brothers who at home on Hillcrest Road conceptualized, combed through the detail, and figured out a way to pitch their idea to the school. And come hell or high water, literally, they'd embark on their big ones in the late spring of '73.

The AT thru-hike as described in the most basic terms was this: jump on the path in northern Georgia and walk the brute a step at a time in more or less a northeasterly direction "thru" to Katahdin in Maine. Along the way were some of the best mountain vistas of North Carolina,

Tennessee, Virginia, Maryland, Pennsylvania, New Jersey, New York, Connecticut, Massachusetts, Vermont, New Hampshire, and a sliver of West Virginia. The length of the trail, 2,197.3 miles last I looked, varies year to year due to route modifications. For the AT warrior on a torrid twenty miles per day schedule, accounting for two weeks of off days for rest and resupply of provisions, as is normal, they'd do well to cover 500 miles in a month. That rounded out to four and a half months of aggressive hiking to reach the northern terminus. Begin a thru-hike in early March and without major delay the fleetest will arrive at Katahdin by late July. The idea behind this timetable was to walk north with the onset of spring and thereby mostly miss any snow in the highest southern mountains. And, equally important, acquire the hiking legs, stamina, fortitude, and climate adaptation to endure summer's punishing heat along the way.[11]

But the less speedy, more typical thru-hiker aspirant would clamber up to Katahdin's craggy, out-of-this-world 5,269-foot summit in late August or September, some five and a half months after departing North Georgia. Even with a sprinkling of "zero" mileage days for recuperation and leisure, that's still a brisk fourteen-miles-a-day average. For the slower travelers, they probably escaped the worst of the northern forest's infamous June/July black fly season. Ultimately, around a quarter of all who start at Springer make it to the end in Maine.

There were other ways, of course, to skin this devilish fourteen-state cat. As Bob would, an emboldened band

---

[11] AT hikers benefit from cooler temps in the trail's higher locations. However, heat along lower ridgelines and in valleys can be trouble. Consider that the mid-trail's 500 miles from northern Virginia to Massachusetts rarely climb to 2,000 feet and cross the Potomac, Susquehanna, Delaware, and Hudson river valleys, and the trip can pack plenty of elevated THI days from May into September.

of hikers could elect to start in Maine. On a persistent yet sane schedule, the southbounder who sets out by Memorial Day can expect to reach the finish line around mid-October. Some benefits to leaving from Maine and walking to Georgia include avoiding shelters overflowing with northbound thru-hikers in the South and navigating some of the trail's most fearsome northern New England miles with fresher legs early in the journey.[12]

Not terribly surprising, the forward-thinking Brugmanns customized their own variation of the thru-hike in plotting their '73 trips. Their blueprint had Bob walking from Maine until he met Jeb, who would start from Georgia. Then, in the remaining weeks before returning to school, Bob would continue to push south, Jeb north, until their timeclocks expired and they returned to the Monday-to-Friday mundanity of HCHS. The brothers' schematic factored into the schedule a meet-up and rest break somewhere in the middle before resuming their solo treks. Being consummate planners, Bob and Jeb might have had additional ideas sketched out and stowed in their packs had anything in their original plans gone awry. Amazing to me is the detail they consumed. They were just two kids, lapsed boy scouts, with this wild idea about something low budget yet ambitious they might accomplish while still in high school.

Prior to the brothers' big hikes, my AT journals documented six trips with the Brugmanns from May '71 to December '72. Our wanderings extended from the

---

[12] In recent years, the administration of the Appalachian Trail Conservancy has pushed an alternate thru-hike plan called the "flip-flop" that has gained traction with today's engorged AT thru-hiker community. It encourages starting at the Potomac in mid-spring and heading north. After reaching Maine, the flip-flopper reverses direction to hike south from Harpers Ferry with the falling leaves to reach Georgia ahead of winter.

Hudson River to almost the Susquehanna, more than 200 miles. With New Jersey and sizable pieces of New York and Pennsylvania in the can, what need would Bob and Jeb have to repeat-hike that mileage in '73? By shaving off approximately one-twentieth of the trail, could they manage modified end-to-end hikes during a compressed three-months-plus timespan? Jeb had also told me in 2022 he'd made two trips early in the spring of '73 that netted him 150 AT miles from Virginia to Pennsylvania while Bob stayed back to work restaurant shifts to save money and push ahead school projects.

While completion of the AT was the Brugmanns' announced goal, their June starts calculated against the reality of 2,000 miles of mountains and a calendar that put them back at HCHS by September begged the question: was an end-to-end hike in a single season, even one trimmed by a few hundred miles, possible? In his professional curriculum vitae, Jeb lists completion of the Appalachian Trail by age sixteen—and the Jeb I know would never take any personal liberty with facts. Yet something doesn't add up. What was the full story here?

20. Bob & Me: The Last Waltz
Flemington and Clark Valley, Pennsylvania;
September-December 1972

As for me, I was still searching for a safety railing at school through sports when I met with Louis Shamsky, Central's Russian teacher and cross-country coach. Mr. Shamsky handed me a summer training schedule to follow and approved my joining the team for the fall 1972 season. While I had acquired some endurance from hiking and shooting hoops and therefore some confidence about my ability to succeed, I knew little about XC other than what a team member said: "Dude, you run two and a half miles all out, up hills and down, and hope you don't pass out or puke when you finish." An unspoken beauty of cross-country is that it is one of the least complicated of all sports. Truly, there's not much of a learning curve: you line up and just fucking run! It's pain and glory for idiots.

I didn't know this then but my clock for hiking with the Brugmanns was winding down as I entered eleventh grade and priorities shifted. Before Bob, Jeb, and I would get out in the woods again, in early '73, I had redirected my surfeit sixteen-year-old energies to the XC team and to building a stronger profile around school—as some brash kid who by keeping pace with the varsity around the fields in our track shorts might catch the eyes of a few girls. It was worth a try.

When my first go at cross ended late that fall with enough athletic success and new social possibilities to feed my cravings, I'd been so absorbed in my own affairs I'd barely paid attention to Bob's and Jeb's. Yeah, I'd catch them between classes or at lunch and we'd chat. But their latest battles with the administration, their work on the McGovern for President campaign, or even their evolving hiking plans were now mostly off my radar.

Bob was further invested in town recycling, developing the curriculum for Central's new environmental course, and proudly held a seat on both the student and community-elected boards of education. (As a student-board member, Brugmann was that group's peer selection to serve as its rep on the big HCHS board. As such, Bob endured hours upon hours of boring meetings but was privy to high-level school business.) In the Central yearbook, *The Echo*, the lone photo of him from that year's edition is the student-board shot. Typical of both brothers, if they felt their appearance in a photo might misrepresent themselves, they skipped out. It seemed Bob attached great importance to his board work compared to his homeroom comrades by his absence from that picture.

In any event, with XC ended by Thanksgiving and my friend now free of meetings and his multitude of other responsibilities, Bob and I mapped out a twenty-eight-miler on the Appalachian Trail that would bring us to within a day's hike of the Susquehanna River.

At this juncture all that remained of my trail time with the Brugmanns—AT activity before the accident—was this bold two-day dash with Bob and a second overnighter the next month with Jeb and Bob as the calendar flipped to the New Year. Both outings, in tough conditions, would test our respective mettles for wilderness travel and build character. Lots of character. And as I learned during these expeditions, nothing—snow, rain, teeth-chattering cold, nor flying bullets—was enough to keep the brothers off the trail. So on December 2, Bob and I risked an adventure to Penn's Woods, thinking we'd sneak in a good hike ahead of winter. It would be our fourth and final AT trip to the Keystone State.

Indeed it was risky. First, the morning we started high up Blue Mountain, we found the footpath covered with three inches of snow. Second, we were heading into the woods, deep backcountry, during PA's holiest of hunting traditions: buck season.

How we got this one approved by Dad and Millie, I don't know. But attitudes back then were different; levelheaded parents like ours' handed their teenagers rope and a permission slip to find their way. Undeterred by the icy footpath, Bob was eager to get out in these conditions; they presenting an opportunity to hone his scout-acquired winter camping skills. I was eager too, if less buoyant. After all, what worthy boy backpacker wouldn't be drawn to the solitude of the frosty mountains and idea of burrowing under the December stars with little more than a sheet of tent canvas and sack of feathers to keep his feet and fingers thawed and penis from turning blue? Adding to the allure was the trail route itself. If anywhere in Pennsylvania right of the big Susie-Q qualifies as being out there, it's this 44,000-acre hunk of game lands known as St. Anthony's Wilderness: said to be the largest roadless area in the eastern half of the state. This was our stage to test our inner Daniel Boone or Jeremiah Johnson.

Though my notes didn't specify how much hunting activity we encountered, enough shots blasted from nearby to motivate us to keep our asses moving. Pretty as the surroundings were, the glittering snowscape turned to slush and before long, goopy meltwater seeped its way inside our boots. We had mud-caked shoes and filthy socks to try to dry out with the limited heat of a campfire on a night with the mercury slipping towards 20°F. Goddamn, it was miserable. Otherwise, we were doing what we came here for and having great fun building up character.

The next morning, despite moisture-wrinkled feet wrapped in damp socks and mucky boots, Bob and I knew what we had to do, the hardened young shits that we were. In silent suffering we punched through eleven miles of State Games Lands #211 to our second night's campsite; in a serene glen close to the end of our journey. We set up the tent near the ruins of the Clark Valley Shelter, built a fire, wolfed down some grub, and crawled into our respective bedroll to go to sleep at dusk. By the middle of the next morning, we finished the walk at lonesome Route 325 and thumbed back to New Jersey.

21. Just Guts
Delaware Water Gap, New Jersey; January 1973

Bob was two months shy of seventeen when we finished the St. Anthony's Wilderness hike. In a year and a half, the Brugmann brothers and I had logged 230 miles of trail in New Jersey, Pennsylvania, and New York. When I view that accomplishment through the lenses of time, I'm struck by one quality we relied on: our guts. Neither Bob, Jeb, nor I had reached the state driving age. But we didn't see what we were doing as anything exceptional. They were simply good challenges that offered us affordable adventure that meshed with our interests, independent streaks, wanderlust, and quests to find a way through the social thicket at HCHS on our terms. Instead of band, football, the stage, or weed, we camped out and did stupendous hikes; from the planning to financing to transportation, entirely on our own. All it required was the guts to pack up and go.

If others saw our expeditions as something special, we wouldn't know. Mom and Dad went along with this vagabonding in their usual hands-off parenting style, viewing me at my core a loner who found some welcome comradeship with the Brugmanns. Though they voiced concerns we could get hurt—break an ankle, suffer a snakebite, get in a car with some psycho hitchhiking—Bill and Gloria must've figured I was okay in the mountains or on the road in the company of these responsible and sensible brothers. Millie, a plucky single mom, was an openly enthusiastic backer of our endeavors, a driver to any trailhead when she wasn't working, and would jump in all the way as her sons' thru-hike supply-line coordinator.

But hiking costs money. Even using secondhand, jury-rigged, or discount-store gear, as Bob and Jeb did, a trip of several months' duration as they'd proposed required a substantial dollar outlay: for two or more pairs of boots, packaged food, the replacement of broken equipment, and transportation. All that plus the coveted (if rare) off-trail motel, restaurant meal, hostel stay, or roadside-stand treat can drain a tight budget to pocket change fast. The only nonmonetary part of a long hike is the free entry to the trail's 2,000 miles of guaranteed adventure and discovery.

Knowing Millie's not unlimited financial reserves—for extra cash, she moonlighted waiting on tables—keeping her sons out there with life supplies and a few bucks in their packs for months would have been a sacrifice. So by saving every nickel from any part-time work they picked up, Bob and Jeb covered most expenses on their own. From our trio's beginnings in '71, the Brugmanns were ninety-eight percent self-financed by their earnings from washing dishes, busing tables, hauling junk, cleaning horse stalls, or picking up local farm work. I got by on restaurant paychecks and a few odd jobs Dad might compensate. We were a very lean operation.

In the touchy subject of money, Millie claimed her former husband reneged on his child-support obligation and didn't help fund his sons' hikes. W. James Brugmann did ad work for auto sales as his day job while living variously in Michigan, Manhattan, Jersey City, and Asbury Park. Along the way he acquired a reverend title and storefront ministry. Mr. Brugmann, whom I had only met at the funeral, had the boys once a month for a dad's weekend but pulled back from that obligation when Bob reached high school and his emerging interests in sports and hiking disrupted the routine.

That business aside, for my final time in the wild with both brothers on the first day of 1973, we rung it in as only Bob, Jeb, and I would. Stemming from their scouting ethic and pumped up by articles in *Backpacker*, the Brugmanns were resolute on mastering the tricks of the trade to successfully winter camp, meaning: carrying everything in on our backs to survive and doing the necessary extras to stay passably warm and adequately provisioned in the event of trouble. They coaxed me to join them and Matt Lee, a friend of Jeb's, for a hike a couple of miles up Dunnfield Creek. Next day we'd continue around Sunfish Pond and exit the woods sometime before dusk.

Well, why not? I'd been at a youth fellowship party the night before, enjoyed some revelry when the ball dropped, and had nothing better to do on the holiday except watch bowl games. With packs stuffed with warm clothes, food, and tents, we were off to the Water Gap.

Dunnfield Creek paralleled the Appalachian Trail and offered a quieter alternative to the busy AT route directly to the pond. Once you get in a few miles, into the creek's upper watershed, we were met with calm as the roar from I-80 dissipated and a wilderness-like solitude prevailed. Somewhere up here we found a dry and level spot, perfect to raise tents. To start a fire, Bob and Jeb tapped into their scouting-manual knowledge to carefully ignite some loose tinder with a single match, noting that had it been our only match—our one chance at survival—we'd have been fine through the night.

It was butt-freezing and toe-tingling cold. Next morning we awakened to snow, which, by daybreak, had transitioned to a numbing thirty-three-degree icy rain. We were out in classic New Jersey winter weather: a little snow to tease and excite, followed by an extended period of rain. A totally sloppy, yucky state of affairs.

However, if anybody could perform in this rot, Bob and Jeb would. After a few misfires that drippy morning they succeeded in getting enough flame going to boil up some packaged oatmeal. After eating, instead of circling Sunfish and adding five shivering miles to our day, we wisely decided to pack up and go home. From a phone booth back at the Water Gap, I called Dad. Had we not been at a heightened risk for hypothermia we'd have enjoyed one of the state's best hikes—a circumnavigation of the ice-coated pond without being bothered by the usual fair-weather mobs who trek up from the parking lots at the gap.

Bob and Jeb, in some of the most adverse weather we'd been out in, were as composed as veteran ship captains in a storm-tossed sea, and very much in command. They had to be as chilled as Matt and I but efficient as ever in packing everything up, nary uttering a swear word, and able to roll with every punch the rawest of January mornings threw us. They were a championship team, a phenomenal partnership. Two kids loaded with fortitude and guts.

We were home by that afternoon, and I would never winter camp again.

22. Brotherly Love
Appalachian Trail, New York to Vermont, 1972;
Flemington; 1972-73

Brothers who were close couldn't always sustain equanimity. We'd argue. We'd compete, often intensely, as rivals. We were capable of hurting the other sibling whether through physical fighting or other forms of provocation. To a malicious degree at times, Ken was my bully and tormentor during our childhoods; then he softened into one of my life's closest companions from age fourteen straight into our thirties. Later, after we married, the relationship settled to a sort of we'll-catch-up-at-Christmas tedium. Months may pass without a word of communication. Sadly, it took Ken's three-year struggle against a lethal cancer for us to regain the robust brotherhood we shared as young men. In a span of five years, as I mourned the loss of Mom, then Ken, then Dad, it was the passing of my brother, on April 6, 2016, at sixty-two, that troubled me most.

According to Jeb, it was June 1972 (one year before the big hikes) when he and Bob left the Bear Mountain Bridge with full packs for Katahdin, two months and 800 trail miles to the north. They'd been inspired to try the six-state walk from New York to Maine after reading *Appalachian Hiker*, the new book based on Ed Garvey's thru-hikes. In fact, Jeb cited Garvey's book as the impetus for the spawning of the modern hiking community's preoccupation with the full 2,200-mile AT journey. Before Garvey, only a handful of dreamers ever viewed the pathway in terms of a single trip; an entity meant to travel from one end to the other. Who would be so bold, or nuts, to try?

Three days after Bob and Jeb set out, Hurricane Agnes churned up the Appalachians and in lockstep with a second low-pressure system from the west, annihilated the interior Northeast states with historic flooding and damage. Although their hiking territory was spared the worst impacts of the storm, Agnes caught up with the brothers in Connecticut and brought the teenage backpackers nine days of monsoon-like travel and soggy camping.

After the two straggled into Massachusetts and the weather cleared, Bob was nursing a worrisome blister. Still, the ever-determined Brugmanns, at ages 16 and 14, willed themselves onward, over 3,489-foot Mount Greylock and into lower Vermont. Bob's condition continued to worsen, however, leaving him limping and his foot now too swollen to fit in a boot. The brothers managed to hobble to Stratton Pond and hole up in the Green Mountain Club camp facility for a few days to see if inactivity might mend Bob. When it didn't, my friend saw a doctor in Manchester, who diagnosed an infected foot, prescribed antibiotics, and ordered the young hiker home on the next bus.

Even when you're getting along and working together, as Bob and Jeb did so well, hiking (or any strenuous long-duration activity) is stressful. Ken and Richie, the fellow whom he paired with to hitchhike to California and back in '71, were the best of buddies when their trip began. When they returned to New Jersey forty days later, they were barely talking. In time the friendship would recover, yet it was never what it once had been.

The Appalachian Trail was a tough nut. Published narratives of long-haulers with subplots of newly minted friends coming together and splitting apart dramatize many stories. Typically, a thru-hiker would find a companion or small pack of pals early on and stick together like family for a period of days, even for hundreds of miles. But when differences in walking speed, off-trail activity preferences, and personalities spawn incompatibility, the hiker would gamely break off and move on, maybe find new trail companions. The thru-hike could then become a months-long merry-go-round of revolving casts of characters who form intense, if temporary, relationships, break apart, and (sometimes) reunite later in the journey.

To my knowledge, Bob and Jeb never fought on their '72 expedition—they were even-keeled kids, disinclined to loud outbursts. And they were best friends. But, the days of incessant rain, poor sleep, unvented tensions, differing opinions, the near-constant hunger that dragged down any long-distance hike, and Bob's compromised health resulted in buildups of stress. When the brothers phoned from Manchester with Bob's update, Jeb requested to continue the hike as originally planned, and Millie granted the younger boy permission. Thus they separated; Bob for home while Jeb would endure another three weeks of hiking to New Hampshire. (With $11 in his pack and the toughest 400 miles of the trail ahead, Jeb's spirits ebbed; he bought a return bus ticket from Franconia Notch. This was in late July and would end his first of three Katahdin attempts in three years.)

Bob Brugmann and Ken Lobb would share a mantle for being the older, wiser mentors to Jeb and me, respectively. Born almost two and a half years to the day before me, Ken and I carried many identifiable family idiosyncrasies without a lot of physical resemblance. Ken held swarthy good looks, girlfriends, cool pals, broad popularity, and a celebrity status from his hitchhiking and work as a star teen reporter for the local newspaper, *The Democrat*. As president of Interact, a fixture in school entertainment productions, and the personality behind the bylines at the paper, my brother soaked in the fruits of youthful acclaim without getting terribly bogged down in the knottier academic business of grades or classes. That was Ken.

Bob Brugmann enjoyed hard-won respect, administrative influence, and a wide likeability at Central without the sweeping popularity that Ken, the jocks, the cheerleaders, and stage and music kids bathed in. Bob attained a quieter recognition through his long and lonely conquests on the AT, his solid classroom work, and his leadership in school and community ecology initiatives. But after hanging tight with Bob for two years, I think I had my fill of the long and lonely.

In junior year, once I gained a foothold in a more visible area of school life, I went all in. I wasn't this born-to-run freak from another galaxy and had my share of bad races and breakdowns despite the occasional victory. But the desire to be somebody at HCHS, for recognition, popularity, and identity, was so internalized that I soon committed to year-round team activity: fall cross-country, winter track, spring track. This resulted in a rolling September to June obligation of practices and meets, folowed by more practices and meets, with short breaks between seasons. As such, my attentions gravitated away from the Brugmanns' hikes. In fact, I would become so detached from the process that the details of what Bob and Jeb had planned escaped me. And with Ken now out of Central and me out from his shadow, I burned to occupy his vacated social role with a style of my own.

Ken's graduation in June of '72 opened elbowroom for me. And in a win-win for both of us, after some bouncing around NYC and home, my brother landed at a small college in Michigan, where his life took off further. Although, as a junior at Central and big brother gone, I was no Kenny Lobb. But with one cautious step at a time, my wade into our school's version of the dating game yielded some hits. I was on-and-off with Lori, my first girlfriend, with other friends with fetching names (Lizzie, Debbie, Cindy, Kimberly) coming into play during our cycles of breakups and makeups.

None of this was easy for me. In fact, it was scary, with a lot of swings and misses along with those base hits. But with practice, mostly gathering the courage to act, I wasn't an automatic out when I managed to ask for a Friday night date.

As for Bob, a girlfriend at this point would be a distraction. The guy had a thru-hike to figure out, a course to develop for faculty and administrative approval, board meetings, restaurant shifts, tough classes, and not far down the road, college to consider. There was no time to monkey around, so he invested himself in things he cared about most. Our views on the importance of dating clearly differed and would become a source of separation.

But back to Ken: My brother was no hiker/camper in the way Bob, Jeb, and I were. Yet Ken's nose for adventure and a willingness to "rough it" as he did all during his hitchhiking trip to California in '71 would inspire us three to take on tougher challenges of our own choosing. As I saw him, Ken was an orb of road smarts and big balls; a modern musketeer in our midst.

"There was a certain mythology about Ken Lobb that came with his writing and hitchhiking," Jeb remembered. "He was a Jack Kerouac with a different twist."

Medicated and resting at home, Bob recovered from his injury. But the airtight relationship the brothers enjoyed till then had been punctured. Jeb remembered a waylaid Bob as withdrawn in the aftermath of the aborted hike, which saw the younger brother outperform the older one. By mid-August of '72, when Bob was ready to get back outside, Jeb sensed he wasn't welcome on his brother's hikes. So they walked separately on the AT in New Jersey, in opposite directions. Brotherly love sometimes hits speedbumps.

As siblings linked by DNA, shared experience, and family bonds, Bob and Jeb bounced back. When the calendar turned from '72 to '73 and we shivered through a January night in tents at the Water Gap, they were back to working in sync, keeping spirits up and all safe. If a rift had developed the summer before, I couldn't tell on this outing. They put on a flawless demonstration of Brugmann-esque teamwork.

By early '73, a hesitant Bob grappling with college options, money concerns, the push to get his environmental course approved, and possibly lingering depression, recommitted to some form of a multi-state AT hike that summer. "I always wanted to do it," Jeb recalled, "but after the injury Bob didn't. Then he changed his mind and wanted in."

Thankfully, Jeb and I have survived long enough to rediscover one another and delve into this opportunity to sort out the facts from fragments warped, bent, blurred, and blended by time. Because while my memories remained reliable when centered on my shared experiences with the Brugmanns, for events that did not include my participation, much had been lost. This includes the troubled '72 New England hike and the brothers' strategies for their summer of '73 journeys.

To our good brothers who are no longer here... Bob and Ken, RIP.

Part Four

Rollout

23. Springing Ahead
New Jersey and Connecticut; Spring 1973

Be it in school, playing sports, hiking the trail, coordinating the local recycling effort, or scrubbing clean pots and pans at the restaurant, I learned to not underestimate a Brugmann. For as mild a temperament as Bob had, this dynamo young man wrapped in boy-scout values knew his rights as a seventeen-year-old student and vigorously exercised and defended them. Having dived into the activism scene at Central, my friend knew his way around the administration, curriculum, and school-board policy. Without being a rule-breaker or screaming maniac, Bob was a thorough and effective change agent. So in early '73, on behalf of her two oldest sons, Millie presented in writing Bob's and Jeb's proposals to hike the AT as an educational venture to Central's upper administration and requested an early exit from school that spring and possible delayed return in the fall.

How profoundly our world has changed from then to now, from looser school-attendance expectations to a fully digitized Appalachian Trail navigational experience. Recent years have seen hikers shatter AT records for fastest end-to-end trips over the trail. But for each of these superstars it's also important to acknowledge that their efforts were aided by iPhone technology and "teammates" of friends, family, and corporate-sponsor reps who would show up in vans at road crossings with all manner of supplies and top-quality replacement footwear and poles. Space-age fabrics, lithe trail-running shoes, and minimalist packs help these quasi-professional fitness freaks to run all but the nastiest miles of the trail. Accordingly, a hardy handful of high-octane athletes have completed the Springer-to-Katahdin journey in sixty days or less, with records challenged and broken annually. That's a mind-blowing thirty-six or more miles-per-day average!

Little of this kind of thinking, let alone equipment and technology, existed fifty years ago. The Brugmanns and I were schooled in the ethos of Benton MacKaye's original 1920s Appalachian pathway concept of heading to the faraway hills to rejuvenate, tramp, camp, chop wood, grow crops, and leave behind the impurities of a festering urban America below the ridgelines. Any mileage-driven, hurry-up hiking was anathema to the MacKaye philosophy of the trail. Naturally, any high-mileage day we could claim appealed to Bob, Jeb, and I as much as any young packer now or then. But to hike the AT as a speed contest as if conducted on a running track or the Bonneville Salt Flats never entered our minds.

Then came along Ed Garvey and his neat little book, *Appalachian Hiker: Adventure of a Lifetime*, in 1971. Edward W. Garvey, a retired government accountant, wasn't the first individual to thru-hike the AT; that distinction belonged to Earl Shaffer, in 1948. However, Garvey's account of his end-to-end hike, published during a fertile period of backpacking interest, helped launch a movement that has continued to grow in the ensuing half-century.

The idea of hiking the full trail from Maine to Georgia, or more commonly Georgia to Maine, caught on with Garvey, and caught on with the Brugmanns.

What Bob and Jeb with Millie's backing asked the HCHS administration was an exemption from school in the final weeks of spring and provisional additional time off into the start of the new scholastic year in September. In their time away, the brothers would hike the AT, if not end-to-end, pretty damn far. School officials could be balky about such requests. By allowing the Brugmanns to set a precedent for approved time off, other teens might request absences for reasons less worthy. But with their clean disciplinary records, good grades, and positions of leadership in clubs and organizations, Bob's and Jeb's wishes were granted. The brothers worked within the system and succeeded in making it malleable for their needs.

Who in HCHS could've denied Bob? He had this talent for bringing skillful organization, sincerity and high standards, and a quiet passion to all his affairs—in school, on the trail, at home, or anywhere. As Paul, the youngest of the three Brugmann brothers remembered, "Bob had this internal plumb line that enabled him to reach the stars."

At sixteen, Bob, with ten or so ecology-infused kids and two faculty members signed on, conceptualized and spearheaded the development of Central's first for-credit course in environmental studies which, pending approval, would be offered in his senior year. This was Bob at his best. He and the equally stellar Jeb were the rare students who could dip their feet into activism, show some recalcitrance, join a protest, remain silent during the Pledge of Allegiance, and still win over the teachers and administration.

Yes, they could do all of that. But they were regular boys too who blended in and battled hard but fought nicely. "Bob and Jeb as teenage boys might get into a little trouble," their mother would say. "But they were respectful of others and never hurt anyone."

Trouble? One time Bob and I skipped school to hitchhike to the shore, to crash on our student council kids who paid a buck to come by bus. The school reported our truancy to our parents. That was the totality of Bob in trouble.

Central's school year languished into mid-June, later if days for snow closings were added to the calendar. What June amounted to at HCHS was a few days for finals, then screwing around for several more of busywork and glorified babysitting until we reached the state-mandated one-hundred eighty days of instruction and they let us out for summer. In my reimagining of spring of '73, Bob would have finished his assignments and tests ahead of the Memorial Day break and bolt for Maine a day or two later, with Jeb to follow soon thereafter to Georgia.

However, my diary entries revealed a somewhat different sequence of events. They verified that on Friday, May 25, 1973, a cross-country pal and I began a hike on fresh AT turf in Connecticut. Jeff Gehrs and I planned the trip around the four-day holiday weekend. Without remembering Bob's start date, it's tempting to think that on the day Gehrs and I began our southbound trek from Salisbury, Bob stood atop Katahdin. Therefore, the three of us—Bob, Jeff, and I—separated by four states, scores of mountains, and hundreds of miles, were walking the same trail at the same time!

The AT route through the northwest of Connecticut offered a delightful green tunnel of ravines, forest, and passages through bucolic villages. Thanks to good notetaking, I have distinct memories of this forty-six-mile tour, which endured some rough moments but finished as planned across the state line in Wingdale, New York, on a sopping-wet Memorial Day.[13]

About the rain: On our third day it arrived in force and lingered into the next. With every stitch of clothing leaking through, Gehrs and I found a laundromat in Kent to duck into and try to figure out where to pitch a tent. In an unplanned moment of good fortune that AT hikers know as a trail-angel act, we met a boarding school student in the laundry who invited us to stay in his dorm and spare us the prospect of an insufferable night somewhere outdoors. Around the time Gehrs and I found dry refuge in a Kent School dormitory, Bob had descended the Katahdin massif 700 trail miles to the north and begun his months-long odyssey to Georgia, or to wherever he hoped to get. Yet if the same soaker that nearly annulled mine and Gehrs's walks through the Connecticut hills tracked to the northeast, Bob too would have been hammered by cold rain as he exited Baxter State Park and entered the Pine Tree State's famed "100-Mile Wilderness" section of the AT. This was not the way to start a 2,000-mile hike.

In a word, problematic would best sum up hiking prospects in far northern New England before the start of summer. Long winters bring heavy snow, tree-toppling winds, and limb-snapping ice to the region. A slow-to-arrive spring would turn miles of trail into bogs of meltwater, massive blowdowns, and boot-sucking muck. In the high country, patches of snow and ice can last till June. As a result, in the loneliest reaches of the northern AT, it was fair to expect bad conditions in the spring and hope for something less bad. The going is chancy and slow; this was true for Bob and true for anybody.

---

13   Jeff Gehrs reminded me five decades later he was a newbie to the wilds. "You talked about these great adventures, the hitchhiking, camping, backpacking," my old teammate said from home in Delaware. "But until that hike I'd never done much in the outdoors. Going to Connecticut to do this was huge."

That was how I reimagined Bob's start from Maine—smacked by the same storm up there that nearly chased Gehrs and I off the trail in Connecticut. Reimagined until I spoke with Jeb in 2021, when a less dramatic picture emerged. In his brother's recollection, Bob was still in New Jersey, packing and finishing up eleventh-grade business, while Gehrs and I soldiered through the Memorial Day deluge to get to a train to home.

As the 1972-73 scholastic year at HCHS wound down, our classmate Dennis Shuman recalled a parting conversation with Bob. When Dennis had a clear idea of what the Brugmanns intended to do that summer vacation—each brother going to opposite ends of the trail and hiking solo—he raised the concern about the safety of their plan. But Bob was reassuring and urged our mutual friend not to worry, because "You're never really alone on the Appalachian Trail."

24. Maine to Georgia: Then & Now
Appalachian Trail

When Bob and Jeb launched their respective thru-hikes, the fourteen-state odyssey was more demanding compared to today. Of course, the twenty-first century hiker would still climb up and down every mountain and cover every toenail-bruising mile. The updated trail route, if altered here and there, was approximately the same length, and about as difficult as it was in '73. Geological change is slow; mountains that have stood for epochs don't smooth out in a span of five decades. Katahdin, Mount Washington, and North Carolina's Nantahalas are every bit as challenging to get up and down today as they were half a century ago.

Yet today's thru-hike experience has radically changed. Due in no small measure to the dazzling and multiple uses of the mobile phone as well as some significant on-ground enhancements, the many rigors and hardships one faces in the four-to-six-month walk aren't quite so many nor quite so burdensome anymore. There's nothing soft about the journey, then or now. But the trail's not as lonely, risky, and austere as it was when Bob and Jeb laced up their boots and ventured into the woods.

Consider first the physical trail itself. The Springer to Katahdin route (or Katahdin to Springer), with modifications, remains in place. When I hiked with the scouts and Brugmanns, however, it was common to detour off the footpath for connecting road walks that might last a few minutes or half a day, before returning to the wild. The roads were tedious, but an unavoidable reality of the older AT. The worst part of this mileage was its scarcity of signage and white-blaze markings to show the route. To avoid wasting hours from getting lost in that age of variable quality maps and no GPS technology was one of our bigger challenges.

Thanks to the federal protection of the Appalachian Trail that arrived with the 1968 National Scenic Trails Act, today's trail is nearly entirely an offroad dirt footpath. In one of AT's greatest of paradoxes, despite being more pinched than ever by resort expansions, growing suburbs, new highways, pipeline incursions, and truck terminals, the trail feels more secluded. That's been accomplished by rerouting it onto strips of NPS-owned corridors. For example, the AT still wends its way across Pennsylvania's intensely developed Cumberland Valley. But by moving fifteen miles of the route from roads to adjacent fields and woods, the trail here is now effectively buffered from the most egregious of the area's new-home developments, interstate traffic, and any other human encroachment you can think of.

Other advantages the modern thru-hiker has the pioneer of 1973 did not:

- **A better constructed, maintained, and graded pathway. Sturdier bridges and better-built crossings of wet areas on elevated planks known as puncheon. Fewer areas plagued by erosion or chronic water problems.** On a 2021 hike on Mount Moosilauke, by reputation one of the AT's most demanding climbs, I was generously aided on the ascent by numerous stone and wooden steps and strips of rebar attached to rocks to hold and help pull myself up. I can't imagine these climbing assists and safety features, here in New Hampshire or anywhere, were as convenient or commonplace in '73.

- **An almost flawlessly marked trail.** Between their use of mapping apps, navigational devices, and improved route markings, no AT hiker today should ever more than briefly lose the trail route.

- **Many more trail angels.** Who? What? These are kindly AT neighbors and friends who leave snacks and water in strategic locations along the trail for hikers to help themselves. Other angels might offer long-haul backpackers rides to towns, or places to stay or camp, sometimes with meals, a shower, and linens included. For a nominal charge, voluntary donation, or nothing.

- **An overall safer and less solitary hiking experience due to greater trail use and the ubiquity of personal communication devices.** Rare now is a trail day without another hiker encounter.

- **Access to comfort services.** Need a ride to town? A motel or hostel reservation? To check the hours of an off-trail bakery, pizzeria, or brewery? Arrange for a car to haul your load up the path for ten, twenty, or fifty miles? Call or text from your cell, and your wish will come true, or your question answered. Hiker shuttle transportation is readily available. Any local person with a vehicle can develop a robust cottage industry carting around AT travelers.

- **Localized weather info a screen tap away.** About to cross an open summit and nervous about an approaching cloud deck? A glance at your phone's weather radar will tell in seconds what you need to know and answer your question about whether to push ahead or wait out a storm. Stunning as it is to consider the numbers of directionally challenged travelers on today's AT, no modern thru-hiker must have the weather or spatial smarts to survive that past generations relied on.

The Brugmanns and other long-haul explorers in '73 knew none of these advantages. This was a time of pay phones, cash transactions, hitchhiking to towns, and heavy-load packing—no exceptions, no slackpacking. And of absolute trust in the fluidity of the USPS and small post offices in places like Damascus, Virginia, and Duncannon, Pennsylvania, for on-time deliveries of resupplies of life-sustaining food, equipment, and cash. Once Millie said her goodbyes to Bob and Jeb at the local bus stop and Newark Airport, respectively, the boys were on their own, fully responsible for their well-being. Good luck, be safe, enjoy the journey. And please, sons, try to call your mother every couple of weeks.

They were two high school kids, ages 17 and 15. In the event of a problem, there was no cellphone.

25. Late Out of the Gate
Maine and New Hampshire; June 1973

June as we knew it in New Jersey brought a swinging rope of weather, sudden shifts from cool to hot, with previews of full-on heat, high humidity, and heavy thunderstorms stirred into the month. On the cusp of the solstice, we've broken out the tees and shorts and can't wait to jump into pools and hit the beaches. Up north, however, I had to believe that any mileage pace Bob thought he could sustain would prove impossible due to bad trail conditions and tough weather. In the mire of springtime in Maine, it seemed likely he'd fall behind schedule—to meet up with Jeb, get to Georgia, or whatever plan he'd configured.

But, this was Robert James Brugmann. Despite his youth of seventeen years and four months, Bob was no ordinary AT hiker. He and his brother, James Eric Brugmann, had the skills, the focus, and the tenacity to go the distance and pull off the extraordinary.

A card from Bob from Mount Washington postmarked on June 25 offered no hint of worry, no alarm bells, just a mention that hiking with two companions across Maine had slowed him down. That happened on the trail when individuals with their own ideas and goals came together for safety and companionship, and hiking speeds adjusted out of necessity. This would be inside the Pine Tree State's 100-Mile Wilderness, by reputation a godforsaken place that's entered shortly after the descent from Katahdin. Yet a veteran thru-hiker told me that aside from it being remote, the Wilderness was relatively free of rugged terrain; a strong kid with fresh legs like Bob would make good time there.

June 25, the postmark date, was a Monday. However, I surmised that Bob arrived at Mount Washington two days earlier, wrote the card, and it sat the weekend unprocessed in the summit post office collection box.

The AT distance from there to Clarendon Gorge, Vermont, where Bob would arrive late on July 4, is 173 miles. It's a bone-smashing hike that includes the sky-high Presidentials, the strenuous Kinsman ridge, Big Moose (Mount Moosilauke), and towering Killington Peak. June 25 to July 4 was ten days, meaning my friend would have to maintain close to an eighteen-mile daily average in very demanding terrain and deteriorating weather. I don't think he did. What seemed more likely was that Bob was on Washington by June 23rd, paused to enjoy the amenities, sent a few postcards, then moved along (if more slowly) through twelve days of often soaking rains to mid-state Vermont.

What's known of Bob's final hundred Appalachian Trail miles, eight days from Moosilauke to Clarendon Gorge, is part speculation and part fact gleaned from people who had some contact with my friend during this time. And anything projected about Bob's hiking ambitions beyond Clarendon Gorge is entirely my speculation and semi-moot in view of the accident.

Nonetheless, had things turned out differently, had the trails been dry, had with a super-hiker effort Bob maintained eighteen-mile days, had his fall of course not happened, after completing Vermont my friend might have reached the Hudson River around July 20. Further assuming a return to the AT in Pennsylvania after skipping all previously hiked sections, a short break after meeting up with Jeb, and awarding himself a rest day about every hundred miles, on that aggressive schedule Bob had a fighting chance of arriving at Springer by the last days of September. In a scenario even less likely, free from injury, burnout, weather problems—any slowdown you can think of—he might have ascended Springer close to Labor Day. *Maybe.*

But by any realistic measure, Bob Brugmann getting to Georgia that summer was never going to happen. Labor Day fell on September 3. We returned to school from vacation the day after the holiday, the fourth. How far into the month could Bob and Jeb play hooky while assignments piled up and HCHS's patience with these two boys walking in the woods thinned? Millie, of course, would have supported her kids' wishes and negotiated more time off for them as necessary.

From Bob's June 5 or 6 start date from Katahdin, we figured out through deduction and math that reaching the Springer Mountain endpoint in '73 was a colossal leap for somebody expected in school by mid-September. Still, I believed that solidly inside Vermont, by the time he arrived at Pico Mountain and turned due south, where the Appalachian Trail merges into the Long Trail, Bob had fallen behind whatever timetable he'd charted. And fed up with the endlessly wet weather, Bob was losing patience, composure, and maybe some clarity anyone would need to safely navigate through the morass that awaited his arrival.

Everything considered, the excessive rain, bad trail conditions, and slower companions included, Bob had made commendable if something short of spectacular progress. But compared to the *Backpacker*-magazine-fueled and possibly naïve Brugmann ideal, a too-sluggish rate of advancement. As Jeb would confirm forty-eight years after the accident: Bob was trying to make time. But not to meet his northbound sibling, nor power to Georgia by some ill-considered, near impossible date. Something else entirely was pressing.

Bob was a month into his adventure when he passed Killington and began an extended descent to Clarendon Gorge, eleven miles down the trail.

26. Plans B & C
Flemington; 1973

The popular story that circulated about the Brugmann hikes among people who remember is that the brothers were attempting to walk the AT end-to-end in a summer. All while the rest of us were acquiring tans at the shore, working some menial job, or sneaking into bars to test the enforcement of New Jersey's new eighteen-year-old drinking law. To make their journeys possible, Bob and Jeb got approval from the school to take early finals and begin summer vacation two weeks ahead of all others. Since the distance of the trail against the brothers' start dates and their hiking speeds were checked, we know—or believe we know—that couldn't be entirely accurate.

Knowing as they did beforehand that a single summer AT end-to-end hike, even one truncated by a few hundred miles, was wildly optimistic, what plans for eventually finishing the trail might Bob and Jeb included in their playbooks?

One, Bob had scored a "senior privilege" from HCHS to take additional time off after Labor Day to finish up, thereby indefinitely delaying the start of his final year. Given his pull with the administration and school board, such an arrangement seemed possible, though, ultimately, unrealistic. What school would say yes to one brother and deny the other when both were equally decorated student achievers?

Two, as Jeb insisted, neither brother figured on finishing the trail in one hiking season—do the arithmetic. Instead, they'd hoof it as far as they could by Labor Day, return to HCHS, and finish up the remaining mileage piecemeal during future vacations; anytime they could arrange transportation and get away. Such a timetable would enable Bob to qualify, officially or unofficially, as a thru-hiker sometime in the spring or summer of 1974.

To earn *official* thru-hiker recognition, Appalachian Trail Conservancy rules specified the hiker must complete the trail within a twelve-month period. Therefore, if this same time limit applied half a century ago, Bob's window to count as a thru-hiker was open until early June 1974, giving him a second much abbreviated season to finish. Therefore, bag every mile he could in '73, then figure out how to do the rest.

The ATC made a sharp distinction between who counts as a thru-hiker or *end-to-end* hiker. The end-to-ender may take years, decades, or nearly a lifetime to log new AT miles over various trail sections or segments, so long as the end tally accounts for all 2,197 unique miles. Should I get around to hiking my remaining thousand, I could claim end-to-end status but not thru-hiker. Within the goal-driven AT hiking community, "thru" versus "end-to-end" is an important badge of distinction that venerates the most diehard tribe of hikers above the legions of mere trail enthusiasts—people like me.

Under time constraints and behind schedule as he seemed, *had* Bob progressed beyond VT Route 103 he might have elected to pass up large chunks of mid-trail miles and resume hiking far enough south in Virginia to give himself a shot at Springer by early September. Why burn precious days crossing the comparatively unexciting ridges and valleys between the Susquehanna and Rappahannock when the big, bald beauties of North Carolina and Tennessee beckoned farther to the south? Then, that fall and into the next year, from home base in New Jersey he could more easily return to hike any remaining unclaimed mileage in Maryland, Pennsylvania, northern Virginia, or elsewhere. And to be official-official, perhaps repeat the 230 miles from New York to PA he'd earlier knocked out with me or tackle the 248 he'd covered with Jeb in '72 coming up from Bear Mountain.

But if he could, at minimum, get to southern Vermont, to Routes 11 and 30 near Manchester, where he'd been forced by injury off the trail in '72, any of Bob's options for how to parcel up and finish the remaining 1,600 miles of trail were better served from there.

It was thirty-two miles from Clarendon Gorge to VT 11/30. Had Bob stopped at Clarendon due to time concerns and the fact that the bridge was gone and taken a bus home, he'd have to return to Vermont another time to fill a trail gap. Including travel up and back, that's a four-day-minimum inconvenience involving transportation costs and a night in a motel to further strain his budget. So Bob's determination to push ahead that fateful July evening, no matter what was going on around him or inside his head—a ticking clock, high water from weeks of rain, other self-imposed pressures—almost certainly entered into his decision to try to get across the flooded river.

I could only guess what Bob was thinking in regards to hiking south of Clarendon. Maybe neither plan I've outlined here to get him to the Georgia finish line—as an improbable single-season thru-hiker or a cut-and-paste sojourner who collects the mileage in chunks within a 365-day window—was seriously considered, as long as *before he went to college* in '74 Bob could claim a full AT. Maybe that's all that mattered: finish the fucker and move on. And by extension, Jeb, a year and a half younger and on his own quest, would reach Katahdin before age seventeen, the end of a second summer, ahead of satisfying his school gym requirement! Jeb and Bob, it well appeared, knew doing the trail, all of it, was a two-year deal but didn't widely discuss it. Maybe because, fueled by their own dreams, one brother or both hadn't fully ruled out an epic single-season thru-hike. But since I wasn't joining them, I hadn't paid attention to what exactly they were thinking.

If requirements this exacting determined who qualified as a thru-hiker and who didn't existed fifty years ago, a part of me wondered how much Bob and Jeb cared. Wouldn't they want, pure and simple, to enjoy the thrills of a total Appalachian Trail experience? Because, really, it was the journey and people along the way they'd meet that mattered. Not meeting the requirements of a thru-hiker designation. If it took them longer than a year and the accrued mileage from the earlier hikes to make that goal, so be it. It was the sense of accomplishment they sought; self-glorification was not their thing. Perhaps also they wished to show that in setting a high bar for their less ambitious pals back in school—as in completing the AT before we could vote, operate a car, legally consume a drink, or sign up for Vietnam—what mattered was effort, responsibility, preparation, and perseverance. Not a person's date of birth. Ask any boy scout.

Two questions nagged me. How did Jeb finish all the AT by age sixteen, as stated in his professional curriculum vitae? And knowing how intensely focused these two guys were, would anything short of a by-the-book thru-hike (all the way within one twelve-month window, or a single-summer 2,000-mile sprint) have satisfied them? Probably not.

Part Five
Circumstances Beyond His Control

27. Katahdin to Washington to Moosilauke
Appalachian Trail, Maine and New Hampshire; June 1973

When I hit the trail in Connecticut in late May with Jeff Gehrs, the Brugmanns were at home, a week or more away from their respective departures. The storm that nearly washed Jeff and I from the path on day three and back to Jersey wouldn't directly impact Bob's hike through 281 miles of Maine. However, the trek across the Pine Tree State could be a mean one: vicious ups-and-downs, high-water stream crossings, thick with mosquitoes, moose-inhabited, and lonesome. While most of the U.S. is basking in summery warmth—cookouts, beaches, bathing suits, ballgames—vestiges of winter, chill rain, below-freezing nights, leftover mud and blowdowns, must be accounted for in any early June hike across Maine's boreal wilderness.

Yet, in some of most demanding conditions found on the Appalachian Trail, Bob, in my estimation, was galloping along at almost eighteen miles per day when he reached Mount Washington, New Hampshire, 332 miles from Katahdin. This calculation assumed he started walking south from Katahdin on June 5 or 6 and summited Washington by the 23rd or 24th.[14]

In the postcard I received from the summit (postmarked Monday, June 25), Bob reported:

> "I'm writing from the top of Mt. Washington. Made Monson in 6 days, but have since slowed down while hiking with 2 other guys. Have hit some tough country through the Mahoosucs, Carter Range & today the Presidentials. Actually, nothing has come close to Mt. Katahdin, which was great. Maybe you can join me later on."

To paraphrase some of this: my friend had blitzed nineteen miles a day to reach the small Maine town that served southbound AT hikers as their first resupply post. Monson is 115 miles of wilderness from Katahdin. Leaving Monson and arriving thirteen days later at Washington, Bob would manage sixteen to seventeen a day across the trail's most fearsome 217 miles while "slowed down" by companions.

Bob had passed, if not exceeded, every test of skill, endurance, and thru-hiker toughness to this point. Nothing he wrote suggested trouble, save a bit of impatience regarding his friends' hiking pace. An amazing start to the journey.

Unfortunately for Bob, after leaving Mount Washington, the weather was about to turn against him. It had been an abnormally rainy late spring in New England already with the worst to come.

◊

One of the unnamed hiking companions Bob cited in his postcard was Richard Judy. A twenty-one-year-old southbound thru-hiker, Eagle scout, and fresh University of Georgia graduate, Judy was walking home to the Peach State before he'd launch a career in journalism and corporate public relations.

---

14   All trail mileages references are current. While the official AT distance varies each year due to detours and relocations, the overall length of the route is little changed since 1973.

He Was Too Young To Die

Judy would reach Springer on October 20, 1973, in 141 days. Four months earlier with Bob, partway to the summit during the notoriously steep climb up Mount Moosilauke (some sixty trail miles and 20,000 feet total of elevation gained and lost from Mount Washington) they stopped at a shelter, the Beaver Brook Lean-to, to get out of the weather and take stock of their situation. "We were hiking in horrible conditions—raining like crazy, hypothermia a real concern," Rich remembered. Here, the older hiker decided he'd had enough for a day—but his younger friend had other ideas. "I need to keep going," he recalled the earnest Jersey kid telling him before vanishing into the trees and alpine fog. It was the last time Rich would see Bob.

Bob and Rich began at Katahdin a day or two apart, met at a shelter in the 100-Mile Wilderness, and would share bunkhouse lodging for a night in Monson. The two then buddied up for the strenuous trek over the trail's roughest miles in western Maine, across the Presidential Range to Franconia Notch, and another grueling twenty miles to Moosilauke. They bonded with a tenderness of brothers. "You could hike with Bob for a few days and it was like you'd known him forever. He talked about Jeb, his mom Millie, his dad, the interesting things he was doing at school." Despite four years of age separation, Rich recalled my friend at seventeen as "amazing" in responsibility and maturity.

For Rich the hike down from Maine was, to borrow a familiar adage from Charles Dickens, "The best of times, and the worst of times." "Bob and I were two young men having the adventure of a lifetime," Rich said. Then came two weeks of rain. "We were seeing weather as bad as it gets, one of the worst times ever to be out there. It was like wading through a swamp—but we were young and slugged through."

Rich recalled that entering the '73 hiking season, fewer than a hundred individuals had been thru-hiker-credited by the ATC[15]. This was the dawn of the age of the Maine-to-Georgia (or Georgia-to-Maine) hike. Despite slim odds of success, as Rich would remember, Bob too might have entertained notions of finishing the journey in one compressed season with one sustained super effort. While Jeb insisted not—their hikes would span two summers—the sense of urgency Bob conveyed to Rich teased an alternate agenda. On his own and separated from his brother by 2,000 miles, Bob might have recalibrated a hiking schedule to get him to Springer early enough in September to satisfy the administers at HCHS, who were apparently flexible with my friend's return-to-school date.

In Rich's judgement, any idea Bob had of reaching the end in Georgia within his narrow calendar window, though "humanly possible," was not especially wise. "There's the factor too of enjoying the [thru-hike] experience," he observed. "I wish that he'd slowed down." Bob, however, was quite driven. "He had fire in his eyes."[16]

Rich had fallen a few days behind Bob and was hitchhiking near Killington when a driver who stopped for the bearded young man advised his pack-toting passenger to be extra careful on the trail. "Maybe you heard," the local man told Judy. "Some kid from New Jersey drowned in the river in the Clarendon Gorge."

Rich knew right away who the driver was talking about and regretted to this day that he didn't try harder to

---

15   Larry Luxenberg, founder and president of the Appalachian Trail Museum, told me this number was closer to fifty. But in 1973, on the coattails of the Ed Garvey book, around eight-five more individuals were added to the rolls of credited thru-hikers.

16   I don't want to press too hard the idea of Bob thinking he'd complete the AT in one hiking season, because I think that was unlikely. However, if Bob could pull off a one-summer thru-hike, he might reap some benefits. Among them: an elevated social position at school; more time to focus on college and pet projects; the satisfaction of finishing the AT ahead of Jeb; and release from the self-imposed pressure he felt to hike the whole trail.

persuade Bob to call it quits on that soaking afternoon back in New Hampshire.

Devastated by the news as he was, Rich resumed his hike and reached a location south of the gorge a few days later. He had ventured off-trail in search of food or supplies and encountered a small pickup truck. In its bed Judy eyed a badly soiled yet immediately recognizable backpack. The occupants of the truck were Millie and her partner, Mike; the pack, Bob's. Rich offered the grieving mother condolences, told her his story about hiking with her lost son, and a friendship hatched. When Rich arrived at the Delaware Water Gap weeks later, Millie took the young adventurer home for a night for a meal and comfortable bed on which to rest.

"I'm a person of faith, and if Millie and Mike coming along in the truck was God's doing, I don't doubt it. It was a moment when we both needed the comfort we were able to give each other."

In his seventies and retired from corporate work, Judy remained closely linked to the AT. He helped launch the Appalachian Trail Museum at Pine Grove Furnace, Pennsylvania, and invested in the Len Foote Hike Inn, a popular hostelry on the approach trail to the AT below Springer. He had contributed to the trail's range of published literature as author of *THRU: An Appalachian Trail Love Story*, a novelization of a thru-hike that embodied a near-literal telling of Bob's 1973 hike and accident. Later and more leisurely, Rich completed a northbound end-to-end hike in sections over fifteen years.

Before his daughter and son set out on their own respective thru-hikes, Judy said he told each of them Bob's story as a cautionary tale. "The AT," he warned both, "can be as dangerous as anything."

28. The Right Turn Not Taken
Shrewsbury, Vermont; July 1973 and August 2017

By glossing over the Long Trail and Appalachian Trail guidebook descriptions, the reader from home cannot know the tough going Bob Brugmann would've experienced in his last days and hours as he worked southward from Killington Peak towards Clarendon Gorge. Bob's 3,100-foot descent, stretched out over eleven miles, might have sounded blessedly welcome for our weather-whipped young foot traveler, now 500 miles and thirty-five days into his trip. But the guidebook narratives understate the trail difficulty, and Bob's traverse through here ahead of his accident would in fact turn savage no thanks to rounds and rounds of rainfall to slam the region.

In the 5.5-mile stretch I hiked in 2017, in dry weather forty-four years after the accident, the AT/LT crosses a "swampy area," a brook that "can be challenging in high water," and nearer the gorge, a "boulder-filled ravine."[17] All the work of a mountain stream called the Cold River, gushing tributaries, and a plunging last descent into the noted ravine from a

---

[17] Trail description text from *Appalachian Trail Guide New Hampshire-Vermont*, Twelfth Edition.

He Was Too Young To Die

prominence known as Beacon Hill, which still sat almost a thousand feet higher than the gorge. To arrive at the road before the gorge, one would first plod through truckloads of water and muck, make a stiff 350-foot ascent, and drop down precipitously over huge rocks. All as it seems Bob had in the immediate aftermath of a historic rainfall. When I walked these miles, I found their steep ups and downs and scrappy water navigations to be intimidating and hated to consider the shoe-sucking quagmire my friend endured when he passed.

Yet hikers will be hikers. Sometimes they'd get stuck in bad stuff, curse, and panic. But they would manage to make it up, down, over, across, or through whatever the obstacle or quandary of the moment might be. A hiker persevered and built character and strength for the next challenge, and the next. Hikers were a determined bunch, disinclined to retreat or quit.

But the hiker also pushed ahead on adrenaline—a dependable source of strength and stealthy foe alike. As tired or discouraged they become during any hike, put in front of them a goal like a mountain summit, shelter, campsite, or a road leading to the comforts of a town, and their internal Sir Hillary[18] aided by adrenaline will usually get the hiker to their day's destination.

I had initially determined that Bob was behind schedule at this point in his hike, hurrying to meet up with Jeb, now in Virginia and streaking north. Hurrying, yes, Jeb would confirm. But not to meet up with his younger brother by some predetermined date or location. Bob was rushing to get to Manchester, Vermont, by no later than Friday, July 6, to catch a bus back to New Jersey to take his SAT exam.

Young Bob slopping through some of the worst hiking conditions one could imagine to get to Manchester (thirty-

---

[18] Edmund Hillary, the New Zealander given co-credit for the first successful ascent of Mount Everest, in 1953.

two trail miles south of Clarendon Gorge) in less than forty-eight hours! Further straining this ambitious timetable, he had known by word of mouth that the suspension bridge at the gorge was washed out in the June 30 storms and the marked detour around the outage would add hours of walking to his already tight schedule.

Under the pressure cooker of a limited window of time, the Vermont Transit bus schedule, and Saturday's Scholastic Aptitude Test three states away, Bob Brugmann emerged, presumably soaked and soiled, from the woods to Highway 103, late in the afternoon of Wednesday, July 4, 1973.

I've long asked what I would've done had I arrived there and found, down an embankment into the gorge, a demolished bridge and one fallen tree dangling over the raging brown water, tantalizingly extended across the void, though several feet short of the opposite bank. *Christ almighty, now what?*

While I'd mastered hiking's basics by my middle teens, I wasn't the pro Bob was. In tasks that demanded perseverance or taking a calculated risk, he was the braver of the two of us. (Stubbornly, Bob stuck with football after I'd given it up.) My friend also outshined me in his comfort in rocky or exposed environments, Lehigh Gap or the Lemon Squeezer. Bob stayed calm when I didn't. Composed in the restaurant kitchen when the dirty dishes piled up or the chef demanded his gravy vats be washed. Cool, confident, always.

Contrary to my timid self, I tended to not be fearful around water crossings when hiking. Specifically, the navigations that entail hopping over small streams on rocks or logs; where the application of normal footwork or balance comes into play. Within perceived safe bounds, I found these crossings fun. Should I slip, so long as there's no clear danger of getting pulled under, swept away, engulfed in cold water, or crushing a body part, I will be fine. No harm in a little water, some dirt, a soggy boot, or even a minor scrape. It came with the territory that is hiking.

What I feared was heights, the condition known as being acrophobic. More precisely, my fear was of edges. Standing on an open mountaintop by itself didn't bother me. However, I could be on a diving board or atop a medium-size cliff shaking and afraid to leap. Friends would laugh. But on exposed high peaks I'm okay if I'm not on the edge looking down hundreds of feet at my imagined fatal fall.

If I arrived at the gorge, demoralized after a bad day, and saw what Bob saw, I think my caution would have won over any fancy for water crossings. To shimmy out on a tree trunk above an angry river, nothing secure in the stream to step on, nothing on the far bank to grab? Edgy stuff. I would have retreated to the highway, found a motel room in Rutland to dry out, regroup, and check on conditions the next day. If the river was still dangerous, the detour too long, I would have headed home.

Had Bob and I, or Bob and another hiker, been there together, would we have been more emboldened—blinded by collective adrenaline rush—to attempt the crossing? Or been smarter in unison and backed off? Working together, could we have conquered the breach? Or both entered the water and perished? Even worse, one hiker makes it safely to the other side while the other doesn't.

I never had to face that decision, alone or with a friend, in that improbable convergence of circumstances as Bob did. Still, the bitter truth is that Bob had a choice. When he reached VT 103, saw the turbulent river in the gorge below and understood the risk in attempting to cross, he could have elected to turn right on 103, and in a few miles found a motel. Worry later about what to do about the rest of the hike and his damn SAT.

How I wish Bob had turned right instead of continuing down the slope and onto that tree.

29. The Night Before
Shrewsbury, Vermont; July 1973

It is highly probable that Pamela Kerstner and her folks were the last people to converse with Bob.[19]

Half a century ago, fourteen-year-old Pam was living in the family trailer home along Lower Cold River Road. "The Long Trail passed ten feet from the house. We saw hikers all the time, and Dad kept a Coke machine in the garage for them to help themselves," Kerstner recalled.

On his slog down from Killington in the catastrophic rains of that summer Bob appeared late on a Tuesday. As Pam remembered, "He was soaked one end to the other and wanted a place to stop and catch his breath." Her family of trail angels, accustomed to assisting hikers, offered my friend a cot in their garage, laundry services, and dinner. Bob graciously accepted all, save the meal. Maybe his decline of dinner was his boy-scout modesty surfacing, or the efficiency-minded long-haul hiker had food in his pack

---

19   My efforts to reconstruct Bob's final days were boosted after I found an item from Kerstner in a GMC story on the Clarendon Gorge suspension bridge and contacted her. A retired aide for disabled persons, Pam lives in Rutland, ten miles from the gorge.

to eat and lighten his load before his next resupply. We'll never know for certain.

But absolutely the well-mannered boy, not much older than she and making his way alone down from Maine, made an impression on the teenage girl. "I thought someday this could be me," Pam reflected. "If I wanted to be a hiker, Bob was the guy I'd look up to."

Next morning, against the advisement of her father, Bob packed up his belongings and proceeded southbound down the trail. "Dad was almost pleading with him to delay hiking for a day. We were shocked when Bob got across the Cold River."[20] According to Pam, the shared Appalachian Trail/Long Trail route Bob would've travelled in '73 from the family home took him on old woods roads to Vermont 103, thus sparing my friend the treacherous final descent through a rocky ravine to the highway and bridge outage, had he followed today's trail alignment.

Bob was better rested and not as much at wits' end as the abysmal hiking conditions of the day suggested. Ordinarily, that's a good thing. But in Bob's anything but ordinary circumstances, if he felt energetic, a little feisty, upon arriving at Clarendon Gorge, that would be dangerous.

By 5:30 PM, with three hours-plus of summer daylight remaining, Bob had covered four miles since breakfast. And if he slept at Governor Clement Shelter three miles to the north the night before his stay with the Kerstners, as Pam believed, the friend I knew would have arrived at VT 103 restless and eager to keep moving after two days of limited advancement.

Pam suspected my star-crossed friend had his sights that evening on Greenwall Shelter, 7.7 miles ahead. But to

---

20   A swift-flowing mountain stream, the Cold and its tributaries crisscross the area and were challenging to ford in normal flow times when I hiked here in 2017.

arrive there before nightfall when you factor in the detour wasn't possible. So Bob elected to cross the flooded river on a fallen tree.

In the isolation of rural Vermont a half-century ago, Pam and her family only learned about Bob's accident from reading about it in the next day's *Rutland Herald*. His was one of several deaths (exact numbers vary) in the state attributed to the historic flooding.

My friend, as she acknowledged, was youthful and ambitious. "But others we saw back then were just as young. Bob was confident and seemed sure of his abilities; but nothing about him was cocky."

Pam and her parents attended the GMC dedication for the rebuilt Clarendon Gorge suspension bridge the next year on August 24. "They told Bob's mom and dad that when their son left us, he was in good spirits and had on dry clothes. Every time I'm down there and walk that bridge, I think about Bob."

30. Lost in the Flood
Shrewsbury and Clarendon, Vermont; July 4-8, 1973

I dread what's next. And in respect to surviving family members, I'll be selective about what I share from what is known after Bob entered the water. (Should you want to know more about search and rescue, and details about local flood conditions, abundant information may be found from newspaper articles culled by the Historical Society of Clarendon, Vermont.)[21]

Accounts inevitably vary, but Bob's engulfment was observed by at least two onlookers: visitors to the gorge, or other hikers in the vicinity, who notified Vermont State Police. As Millie told it, the tree on which Bob attempted to cross the breach extended to about six feet from the far bank. Between Bob and safety, the main current of the storm-enraged river surged below. Had he attempted to leap tree to bank from a standing position with a loaded pack, he'd almost certainly land short. It's also possible, if unconfirmed, that my friend had eyed a rock in the stream he might bound to, steady himself, and jump again to the

---

21   www.clarendonvthistory.org

other side. Another explanation that circulated is that as Bob shimmied out over the roiling floodwaters on the tree, he simply slipped and fell and was pulled under by the weight of his pack.

Millie remembered Bob being a strong swimmer, so he likely had confidence in his ability to enter the torrent in the middle of the void and scramble a few feet to land. Of course, whatever crossing strategy he chose was unsuccessful. And once in the maelstrom of the Mill River, Bob had little chance of escape.[22]

Home early that evening on Hillcrest Road, Millie was preparing a holiday meal for Mike and her youngest son, Paul, when she or Mike answered a call from the police in Vermont. A backpack was found approximately half a mile downstream from where witnesses saw a hiker enter the water at Clarendon Gorge and carried away about 5:30 that afternoon. Contents inside the pack identified the owner as Robert Brugmann of Flemington, New Jersey. A search was underway; the hiker remained missing.

In a frenzy, Millie, Mike, and Paul up packed and drove to Rutland; arriving late in the evening to find the area in post-flood havoc: roads closed, bridges gone, detours everywhere. And no new information about the lost hiker.

The next morning, as search and rescue resumed, Millie confirmed the recovered pack as Bob's.

Jeb, who'd been hiking in Virginia, was in a post office near Roanoke to collect a resupply box when he received a message to call his grandfather, George Nutz. They talked. A flight to

---

[22] According to Tom Broido, an ex-Green Mountain Club employee who helped rebuild the Clarendon Gorge bridge, the Mill River bends just before it enters the gorge. This can result in backups in high water conditions that periodically dump their overloads downstream. It's possible, Broido said, when Bob saw and judged the river safe to cross and proceeded, a fresh torrent of floodwaters and detritus arrived as my friend was in mid-navigation.

Albany, New York, was arranged and Jeb soon joined Paul, Millie, Mike, and rescue personnel in a grim search for the missing and now presumed drowned young man.

Four days after the accident, Bob's remains were found more than two and a half miles downstream against a railroad bridge abutment in Clarendon. Cremation took place in Troy, New York.

From the days after the accident to the present, family members and others who knew Bob laud his good judgment to release his pack after he entered the water, to give himself his best chance to stay afloat and reach safety. That was the boy scout in Bob coming through, in his last, desperate minutes. He had also, it seemed, thoroughly packed and sealed his personal contents (camera, wallet with ID, journal) in anticipation of a wet trail day—or worse, as things turned out. All survived the inundation and were recovered. To his very end Bob had honored the scouts' motto, "Be Prepared," and the volunteer scoutmasters who instructed him back in Readington.

Naturally, shock waves followed. One of my worst moments came a day or two after the accident with the delivery of Bob's postcard from Mount Washington, ten or eleven days after its June 25th postmark. "Maybe you can join me later on," he'd written. In spirit I would—many years down the long trail of my own life.

Filled with almost unbearable survivor's guilt, Jeb would go into hiking overdrive and enter therapy. "I was in bad shape for five or six years, a wreck," he told me decades later.

Millie, desiring to live up to her fallen son's reach-for-the-stars standards, would leave her well-salaried corporate position to retrain as an end-of-life nurse. She gave up her horses, took up hiking, and moved to Vermont. After a later move to the Midwest to be near Paul and her grandchildren, she returned to the Green Mountain State a second time at age 80. Drawn back to this beautiful place, she said, to feel closer to the son whose remains were scattered along the trail he found his greatest joy.

Just weeks after the accident, on his invitation, Jeb and I were back on the Appalachian Trail, crossing the White Mountain National Forest with lots on our minds but not much to talk about. Thinking, I suppose, the superabundance of nature's gifts there might ease the enormity of our losses: of brother and best friend.

Jeb and I made excellent teammates in New Hampshire, but when he returned to the AT later that same August to hike from Monson, Maine, to Katahdin, the trail's northernmost 115 miles, he'd hit a snag. The plan, he recalled, was to meet a companion he hiked with earlier that summer in the South. But after waiting two nights in a shelter for the friend to arrive, Jeb gave up and went home. This was his second failed bid in as many summers to reach the fabled mountain. He was back at HCHS for the start of junior year, on time with the rest of us save Bob.

31. In Bob's Defense
Clarendon Gorge, Vermont

Although he made the wrong decision, I defended my friend for his decision. It was the hiker inside of him speaking; the self-assured adventurer who had already adroitly handled dozens of challenges in 500 miles coming down from Maine; gaining confidence and skill with each successful negotiation of each intimidating ledge and rockslide. What's one more hairy water crossing for this terrain-tested long-distance trekker to ford? Hiking, as any skill activity, builds on itself. On a foundation of muscle memory and confidence. When you hike more, you hike better.

But under internalized pressure to keep moving his hike along, Bob made one miscalculation in conditions perfectly aligned against him, and it cost him. Forget that he was seventeen, or any other claim he was too young to do what he was doing. That's rubbish.

The thru-hike majority I see on today's AT is young and rock-star athletic. On hiatus from future responsibilities; treating themselves to a big bash before sinking into things less exciting (grad school, career, family, house, etc.) that would preclude them from taking four-to-six months away from life to walk 2,200 miles. Others I see in fair numbers appear to be ex-military people and other transitional folks doing personal warfare against some trauma, addiction, or incarceration, walking off the pain; mostly under age forty. Less common is to encounter somebody like me—sixty-five-plus club hiker, trying to accomplish something very significant before worn-down body parts strip away opportunity. And never do I see a Bob or Jeb Brugmann. What a handful of gutsy teens back then engaged in is gone. In a world that has become culturally and conscientiously more protective and less inclined to put grownup expectations on the young, kids don't do stuff like this anymore.

A stickier question to ask is this: Should Bob have been alone? There were risks, for sure. But looking at this question from the time period and a hiker's point of view, I defend Bob, the brothers' decision to split up, and Millie's OK to allow her sons to venture into the wild, such as they did. Bob and Jeb had the tools—maturity, skill, tenacity, common sense—to strike out separately and be safe and successful.

Does today's twenty-four-year-old thru-hiker have a trail aptitude—knowledge and judgment—better than my friends did at seventeen and fifteen? I don't suspect so. (Better technology, financial resources, and payment options, without any doubt.) But any suggestion to me that the Brugmanns were too young, too inexperienced, too far adrift without supervision, doesn't fly.

Overall, travel up and down the Appalachian Trail is safe. Yet if you make one mistake or misstep in the wrong place, time, and conditions, you can die. That's no different than getting nailed by a speeding car anytime I cross the busy street a block home while walking my neighborhood.

Bob was unlucky. Period.

Part Six

Life Goes On

32. July 4-5, 1973
Stanton, New Jersey

With the exception of Thanksgiving and Christmas, holidays never mattered a lot to the Lobbs. Traditionally, beaches or pools, cookouts, parades with firetrucks, old soldiers, and school bands mark a Jersey Fourth celebration. By '73 we'd given up all that. "Too goddamn crowded at the shore," said Dad. Too hot, too humid, too buggy for Mom to comfortably get outside. Heck, we hadn't been to a public fireworks shoot in years. Instead, Dad, ex-serviceman and war vet, would hang an American flag off the porch and grill burgers while Mom fussed in the kitchen mixing a potato salad and boiling water for corn. Uncle Merv, her brother, might join us to eat, nap, and catch a few innings of an afternoon doubleheader. The next day, Dad would return to work and take Ken, whom my father employed that summer for odds and ends in home construction.

For me, I was having a different sort of summer vacation: my last as a high school student. Off-kilter, perhaps, yet not all bad. Through HCHS I took the driver ed course in anticipation of my seventeenth birthday (the state driving age) on July 28. I was at the restaurant a few nights a week, but due to a change in ownership, most of the old crew had moved on. I was running five miles a day, sometimes more. With two of the new guys at work, college freshmen named McCabe and Thoma, we travelled to Rider College for informal evening track meets. On our second trip down, I came close to winning the two-mile. I had started to believe I could be good at this stuff.

One thing in low supply was friends. Bob and Jeb, of course, had been hiking the AT for a month, with no word yet on their progress. Also MIA were neighborhood fixtures Brock and Larry Collins—away at their cottage at the St. Lawrence River, or caught in the tempest of a family crisis with the breakup of their parents' marriage. I played softball an evening or two a week with kids from the Stanton Church youth fellowship, who I remember as being more intent on hooking up and getting high than catching or hitting the ball. Since I wasn't doing a lot of either, I suppose the frustration of sucking at softball hit me harder. Ken was home till late August, with a car. We'd cruise the county, with his buddies and girlfriend, to movies, ice cream stands, or New York to see the Yanks for seventy-five cents for a bleachers seat. My late brother bailed me out a time or two by escorting me around with girls in his snazzy Vega, a Chevy compact marketed to younger drivers.

The weather felt off too. The days ahead of the Fourth brought us one thunderstorm after another: drenching rain followed by broiling sun and humidity, followed by more rain. The kind of oppressiveness that made me ask how summer ever became so popular. Lawns and weeds were growing gangbusters at a time when the July heat normally baked the grass brown. Still, not as crazy as in New England, where we had heard that due to some stalled front, the rain was coming down in insane amounts, with

He Was Too Young To Die

widespread measurements of six to nine inches. Roads washed out, bridges destroyed, railroad tracks ripped up. A bad scene up there.

Despite the warts of daily life—days lazed away with TV reruns, parents pissed off by bored homebound kids—this was the seventies, and the tunes were decent. I attributed my inspired romp around the Rider track to the noise blasting from the stadium speakers, Billy Preston's "Will It Go Round In Circles," as I circled the field eight times. Earlier that year, a new star who'd been creating a buzz around the shore bars released his first LP, that with the vintage Asbury Park cover art. And McCabe and Thoma, fans of Kiss, got me listening to a higher-energy sound. So hello to Bruce Springsteen, Gene Simmons, and Alice Cooper; bye-bye Paul Simon, Cat Stevens, and Glen Campbell.

By the morning of the fifth, the sun finally came out and the rain had gone. I was playing Paul McCartney's *Wild Life* album when the phone rang. We had two extensions in the house, the kitchen and upstairs in Mom and Dad's bedroom, next to the room Ken and I shared. Mom picked up from the bedroom.

I heard her greet Nora LeClair, probably calling to rearrange the weekly bridge game around the other ladies' vacation plans. Mrs. LeClair worked at the school as secretary to the HCHS board. Moments later came Mom's cries and oh-no's, and I lowered the volume. Did something happen to one of Nora's sons, Robbie or Billy, buddies of mine from youth fellowship? To her husband who drove a tanker truck? Next I heard Vermont, bridge, flood, fall, hiker, and from my mother's intonation and shrieks I knew it, I instinctively knew it before I was told what the call was about.

Bob was dead.

Leave it to my beleaguered mother, Gloria, who suffered all her life from anxiety and other neuroses, to report to me what happened, after she hung up with Nora LeClair.

The accident was late yesterday afternoon on July 4. Stream flooded, bridge knocked out, and Bob Brugmann, age 17, tried to cross on a fallen log. Pack found, body lost, boy presumed drowned. Looking for the other brother, Jeb, hiking the Appalachian Trail somewhere down in Virginia.

It has been said the young are resilient, and maybe that's true. Or perhaps at fifteen, sixteen, or seventeen we hadn't experienced enough life to process finality. Jeb was located near Roanoke and in the coming days Bob recovered downstream and cremated. As for the rest of us, life, if briefly turned upside down, continued. I worked restaurant shifts. Ran. Got my driver's permit from the state and some behind-the-wheel practice. Palled around with Ken. Played more softball. Even took my SAT. When you stay busy, even with the mundane, there's less opportunity to think and mope.

Yet for much of the month, until I left for New Hampshire with Jeb after my birthday, I was in a haze. Mom and Dad, to their credit, tried to say kind things and be understanding. A service for Bob was arranged for one evening at Stanton Reformed Church.

Millie and the boys were not churchgoers. However, with Bob's ties to the youth fellowship, the family asked Reverend Miller to host the event with nominal religion doctrine. Mom, a musician at the church, was asked to play the piano. The place was packed.

Nicely call it a commemoration, memorial gathering, or celebration of a life. But there was no getting around this numbing fact: We were going to a funeral without a casket. Mollified only by it by being a midsummer night and lightly infused with end-of-life preacher-speech. Still, one couldn't prepare for the sobbing, the handshakes with strangers, the awkward hugs, and intense sadness. Bob had far more friends from school than I ever knew—the ecology kids, National Honor Society, and student government types came out by the dozens, as did teachers and administrators. So did the youth fellowship and people from the restaurant, including Lizzie. Cherie Nordstrom too. Mom induced additional reflection, if not sorrow, with her rendition of "Bridge Over Troubled Waters."

Millie and Jeb managed to bull their way through the proceedings composed. I couldn't imagine how. Not so much Paul. The youngest kid, headed to ninth grade, looked hopelessly lost and shaken to the core. Propped up just enough to attend by both sets of worldly wise grandparents, the Brugmanns and Nutzes.

I met Wallace James Brugmann, father of Bob, Jeb, and Paul. I hadn't heard many nice things about Mr. Brugmann but remembered him as warm and gracious. He might have been the loneliest person in the church that night.

In the whirlwinds of the evening I missed Millie's invitation for friends to gather at Hillcrest Road after the service. But Terri Clerico remembered going to the house with a boy who was close to Jeb. "We sat with Jeb in his bedroom," Terri's teen posse having strategically spaced themselves from Millie, Mike, and the relatives. "Sat there, barely said a word." As Bob's closest friend, and an object of attention at the church, I slipped out as quickly as I could for ice cream with the fellowship kids. A shake from Round Valley Dairy Treat was all I could swallow.

33. Back In School
Flemington; June 20, 1974

The night we got our diplomas out on the football field, Central recognized three members of the class as posthumous graduates: Bob Brugmann, Debbie Margolin (homicide), and Kathy Marion (vehicular manslaughter). All died in terrible, violent circumstances. At least in my friend's case we could take a small measure of consolation in the fact that Bob made the decision to risk the river crossing. His ensuing struggle was against the insurmountable forces of nature and only nature. One thing all three classmates shared: They were too young to die.

As surely it does and must, life went on after Bob.

My senior year at HCHS saw improving grades, good moments and bad with girlfriends, driving, and a fall weekend to Ken's campus in Michigan highlighted by a double date to a movie. If this was college, a few classes, a bit of study, and fun around every turn, I knew I would continue my education, somehow, somewhere.

My pursuit to become a state champion runner was a bumpy road of surges and stumbles. As soon as you thought you were good, some injury or other health matter would trip you up and you'd be back to zero. Around this time, Central's reliably winning cross-country and track teams entered a period of decline owing to coaching changes, graduation losses, and athletes siphoned away by the school's new lacrosse program. I suppose it was more fun to fling around a ball and knock opponents on their asses than to run two miles and get sick. Just like that, it all fell apart.

As for Bob, he should have been with us winding down our four years at HCHS by wrapping up unfinished business and maybe winding up his social life. His departure felt as if a crater had opened and taken my zest for hiking and any other fun we shared into its hole. For the first time since Mount Mansfield in '69 I had no motivation to hike: Appalachian Trail, Cushetunk Mountain, anywhere. Jeb was around, but only in glimpses: a hallway hey, an impromptu shoot-the-shit within the safety net of mutual buddies—that's about all I could remember.

With track in free fall—Coach Shamsky on sabbatical, the state's eighteen-year-old drinking age diverting the attentions of the team, apathy settling in—I went on a rampage. In an op-ed piece in *The Lamp*, I jumped all over the drinking crowd, the substitute coaches for their lax attitudes, and the locker room indifference killing us. Some teammates were angry, while others supported my position. This was my first stab at activism. It was scary, I bruised some egos; but I would never again relegate myself to sideline silence. I had an epiphany: When something is wrong, find conviction and do something about it. Alas, I would rudely learn later in life that department heads, corporate bosses, and academic deans, even should they ask, don't necessarily want to hear what some minion with other ideas down the chain of command has to say.

I stepped outside my comfort zone to learn transcendental

meditation. For thirty-five bucks, a triad of mellow young men working out of a house in Flemington offered instruction in this ancient artform. Dad was suspicious of anything originating from India and promulgated by hippies, but relented and allowed me use of the car to go to the weekly sessions. To attempt to bring my very jangled head into focus, I learned meditation.

As for college, I applied to one, made a campus visit, got accepted, and enrolled. Just like that. No trips with Mom to tour schools of interest; no involvement from Dad at all except when the bills arrived. I would major in outdoor recreation management at a tiny college in Vermont two and a half hours from the gorge.

How influential was Bob in my turn to activism? In my experimentation with a novel approach to head management? In my college selection and decision to major in a field of study that might make me a park ranger? Maybe some, maybe a lot. Maybe only in my re-imagination.

In that scathing newspaper piece I took an unpopular position to address a situation that ripped at my heart, knowing I'd be subject to scorn and create division. In going against the grain of my cautious upbringing, by learning TM, I entered unknown territory in an attempt at self-improvement—trying a method more in line with the philosophy of the Beatles than the Lobbs. When, junior year, I began perusing college catalogs in the HCHS guidance office, there was this period when I thought I'd go into forestry, same as Bob. But when I looked deeper into that option, at the math and science requirements, there was no way. Next best thing, I'd go to school almost to Canada to become a guy who manages a campground or maintains hiking trails.

Bob's influence? Definitely present in my college decision. Likely a factor in my step into activism to funnel anger and demand change. Possibly in my openness to try meditation—which I needed badly to steady myself eight months after my closest friend died in the most goddamn horrible way one can imagine.

34. Cherie & Joe & Carole & Joel
Cary, North Carolina; Los Angeles, California; Frenchtown, New Jersey

Tracking down Cherie Nordstrom decades later in North Carolina, giving her a key role in our story, and recalling her in the context that I have—as Bob's girlfriend—was tricky and required of me a leap of faith and memory trust. For her part, Cherie more coyly remembered Bob as a "good friend" and part of a tightly knit pack of unattached buddies of mixed gender at high school. Did they pair up as romantic partners for at least a time and engage in something resembling early-seventies 'tween dating: movies, school dances, soda-and-ice-cream outings? Clumsy affection when nobody was looking?

Maybe a little, but mostly not. "Neither of our parents were the types to drive us to the other's house or pick us up from afterschool activities," Cherie insisted. However, on the eighth-grade class trip to the Statue of Liberty and to see *Hello, Dolly!* on Broadway, charming Cherie and gentleman Bob sat as a couple would on the bus, in the theater, and at dinner. Meanwhile—talk about being envious of Brugmann's luck—my seatmate was jabbering

George Hill, rambling and goofy as always.

As I clearly recalled from a hike, Bob was crestfallen when he revealed to me that Cherie had started seeing another boy. This was Ricky Kulp, she confirmed; a dreamboat of a kid with a guitar and sweet voice who performed the songs of James Taylor, Bob Dylan, and Crosby, Stills and Nash at HCHS assemblies. Ricky was immortalized in the yearbook as our Class Singer.

Cherie entered Readington in eighth grade as a new student and found with Bob a safety net. "His parents, like mine, were not together, which was more unusual back then. That's how we first bonded." Their main form of messaging, she further recalled, was the writing and passing of notes. After any period of amorous activity passed, their friendship continued to flourish, and respect deepened. But if Bob had thoughts of reconciliation with Cherie down the road, we'll never know.[23]

Cherie was at a summer school class when the news about Bob arrived. Later, upon meeting up with another HCHS pal to drive to their retail jobs, she shared with him what she'd heard. "He was devastated, and collapsed in grief in the back seat," Cherie remembered.

This was Joe Kohanski, a high-energy trombone-playing classmate Bob knew from student school board.

◊

"Like everyone else at the church that night, I was in a daze, trying to figure out what the fuck happened to Bob," Joe recalled of the memorial service.

My impressions of Joe back at school were of a frenetic,

---

[23] When I asked Bob's mother about his connection with Cherie Nordstrom, Millie couldn't place any girlfriend. When I told her Bob and Cherie had formed an attachment during eighth grade that continued into high school, the older woman welled up and said, "I'm glad he had that experience."

tenacious, super-bright firebrand. If you didn't know him well, as was my case, you still heard him in the cafeteria and felt his impulses around the building. He was the ally who had your back against the punitive forces of the gym class tormentor or authoritarian vice principal, even if your respective social circles mostly separated you from him.

Kohanski was another friend from areas of Bob's school life that by eleventh grade I had become detached: student government, hallway activism, and curriculum development. A musical talent who would record and tour internationally with soul artist Teddy Pendergrass, Blondie, and others, Joe saw Bob as a fellow soldier in the trenches in battling the HCHS administration for our rights and privileges. For example, they took on the big boys—and won approval—for kids seventeen and older to smoke in designated outdoor areas. Bob, of course, deplored tobacco use, but supported the right to smoke, especially as a vehicle to move illicit cigarette use and its airborne carcinogens out of school lavatories.

Upon meeting as sophomores, "I had a sense of who Bob was, that he was my kind of guy," remembered Joe, who transitioned to a law career in Los Angeles after the ubiquitous use of synthesizers curtailed his instrumental opportunities in music. "He had a nose for finding the sources of power in the school, and figuring out how you got things done."

Joe saw Central's jock-worship culture as hostile to non-athletes so he reacted by growing long hair and befriending and defending others: performing arts folks, student government grunts, Vo-tech and farm kids. "We were a big school, transitioning from rural to suburban, and a lot was going on. I had an entrée to a lot of different groups without being part of one clique."

While Bob's voice wasn't the biggest in the room, as Joe pointed out, our friend didn't budge from his values and was thoughtful and thorough. "He was intense, had a great sense of clarity, and would've never made the sell-out move to the administration—or to the oil companies had he been an environmental lawyer."

The accident, Joe lamented, short-circuited his opportunity to form with Bob a deeper, lasting friendship, which at the time was only gaining traction.

Joe's not been to Clarendon Gorge, and never ever made a strong connection with Jeb. Like most of us from that time, he's moved on from '73 but would still think about Bob and reflect. "He would have been a high-end professional in whatever his selected field."

◊

For Joel Boriek and Carole Pepe, Bob was a friendly peer whose scholastic and extracurricular interests at school would sometimes overlap with theirs. Then Bob died. Much later Joel and Carole would make a stunning discovery about their old classmate.

Friends from our HCHS class of '74, Joel and Carole would pair up after college and marry by 1980. Joel and I go back to fourth grade. By eighth grade he, Bob, and I were soccer teammates. Several times in both middle and high school, Joel recalled he and Bob sharing homerooms, classes, and activities such as German, science, and student council. While never on a best-buddies level with Bob, Joel remembered my old hiking companion as "always solid in school and way more serious about student council than I was."

Carole was acquainted with Bob from their shared experiences in Central's outing club, the Challengers. Led by an energetic jack-of-all-trades teacher, coach, and guidance counselor, Frank Osmun, Challengers introduced adventure-inclined teens to thrilling activities such as rappelling, whitewater sports, and outdoor survival. It served as a training course for future participation in Outward Bound.

About a decade after Joel and Carole were together, during a summertime trip to visit her brother, the outdoorsy couple were encouraged by family members to check out a nearby river with a swimming hole and hiking trails in Vermont.

"I could only remember that Bob's drowning was someplace in New England—I didn't know where," said Joel. "When Carole and I got to the river, it was crowded; then we saw the bridge with the sign and couldn't believe it. This also happened to be the anniversary date of Bob's accident."

Carole's recollection of Bob in Challengers raised a good question. If he and I were close friends and on the Appalachian Trail logging twenty-mile days, why hadn't I followed my pal into the boundaries-stretching excitement of the HCHS Challengers group?

Most likely, I think that my raw insecurities stopped me. Namely, the previously referenced acrophobia and fear of exposing low competencies in my use of technical equipment. Hanging against a cliff on a rope I didn't understand how to maneuver or shooting rapids was outside of my comfort zone. Straight ahead hiking or running to exhaustion—that type of fun I could hack.

Joel advanced to varsity soccer captain at HCHS and played competitively into his fifties. Carole, a former special education teacher, ran track when few girls dared. Both are avid bicyclists. As a retirement gig from his work as a wetlands-specialist surveyor, Joel developed and maintains several miles of foot trails in public preserves and parks near his home in Frenchtown.

Joel remembered he was playing baseball with friends at the school field in Three Bridges the afternoon of July 5, 1973, when the terrible news reached him.

35. New Journeys
Vermont, Pennsylvania, Maine; 1974-2024

The Bob Brugmann Memorial Suspension Footbridge at Clarendon Gorge opened on August 24, 1974. In a ribbon-cutting ceremony hosted by the Green Mountain Club, scores of hikers and bridge builders gathered with guests from Bob's family. To remember my friend who perished here fourteen months earlier and to salute the efforts by those who made the reconstruction of the graceful walkway over the Mill River a reality. An article about the bridge dedication in the GMC publication *The Long Trail News* reported the structure being thirty-five feet above the water and seventy feet long between towers. It was a substantial piece of construction that's remained standing for half a century. Withstanding assaults from Hurricane Irene (2011), Sandy (2012), the July 2023 rains, and other storms surely intensified by increasing atmospheric carbon levels and warmer temperatures.

    I was in Vermont at the time of the dedication, but not able to attend. Farther north, I was starting college. Going through the indoctrination agony we knew as Freshman

Orientation. From shared cultural tics and familiar speech, I'd identified other displaced Jersey kids; and together we spent the five days bemoaning what we missed from home and wondering how we'd last for four years in this hippie enclave seven hours from everything we'd known.

Sixteen months later, I packed up and left Lyndonville in the rear mirror; relinquishing teen notions to become a ranger or conservation officer. Mom and Dad picked me up from the dorm and agreed to a detour off the interstate so I could see the site of Bob's accident. It was a ten-minute stop, somber, viciously cold, then back to the car. We were going home for the holidays, to be followed a month later by my enrollment at a second college three states away.

The modest success and notoriety I tasted from high school running would be enough to tilt my decision to change colleges and would influence the course of my life for decades ahead. I was all in with the running, and mostly out with hiking.

Indeed, I ran a ton—first as a HCHS Red Devil, then as a MSC Mountie, later yet as a sort of itinerant marathoner. But in all honesty, I had no identifiable genetic gift for this form of punishment, none at all; just an unquenchable desire. That same burn for identity and recognition—to be good at something; the best I could—trailed me from high school to college and beyond.

Was the running an obsession? Did I become myopic in a single-dimensional pursuit of athletic idealization through a 24/7 devotion to workouts, vitamin supplements, and a plant-based diet, abetted by endorphin addiction? No, not quite. Despite having passion in abundance and a change from one school that did not offer intercollegiate cross-country and track to one that did, I held on to a delicate balance and wider interests, if edging close at times to running's periphery. In spite of instincts to take it into unsafe territory, I was never an extremist. Not in running, hiking, collecting baseball cards, books, the *National Geographic*, or Springsteen recordings.

But as my commitment intensified, a transformation followed. I trained every day, sometimes logging 100 to 120 miles in a week, and raced in community events near to where I attended college. The region there is known as the Endless Mountains, or God's Country. It's the part of Pennsylvania that gets culturally mixed up with Alabama—but for a runner, one couldn't have done a lot better. By hitting the hills, which are everywhere in all varieties of grade and length, he could build deep reserves of endurance; and from these storehouses of stamina and strength, speed follows. If he/she/they can endure the rigors of the mountains, running them is a simple methodology for success.

Meanwhile, my accomplishments from the Appalachian Trail, as in tallying almost 300 miles before I drove a car, receded in importance. Had the fallout from Bob's misfortune helped to precipitate so complete a shift in focus? For perspective, I would consult an old philosophy major.

According to Jeb Brugmann, a spinoff of the back-to-nature movement that had galvanized him, his brother, and me to seek spiritual communion in the woods, would help set in motion the explosive growth in popularity of running that followed the 1972 Olympics. Quite possibly, Jeb surmised, I was swept into this updraft when I crossed over in mid-high school from backpacking and recycling bottles with him and his brother to cross-country and track. And down the road, to competing in marathons.

"Backpacking was the hippie thing to do in the sixties," observed Jeb. From its roots in the counterculture, a subset of the hiking crowd would cross over into running. Not dissimilar to backcountry exploring on two feet, collecting miles in gym shorts and first-generation Nikes was about individualism, low impact, perseverance, and getting oneself closer to nature. And for the purest of the disciples, keeping the brain and body free of the intoxicating liquids and the mind-altering chemical temptations of the day.

When I transitioned from bounding down trails to striding ahead in Waffles, embedded in this culture was a palpable streak of the nonconformity Jeb had alluded to. It was your Prefontaine hero-worshipper longhairs and a few earthy girls who tended to run cross-country, load on the miles, and lead the march into the oddball distance-running phenomenon.

And on the heels of three years of concentrated training that began when I signed up for XC and track at MSC, I found a pathway to the marathon. Much of my collegiate running career, not unlike high school, was a rollercoaster of breakthroughs followed by meltdowns. I was a living model for being consistently inconsistent, which was exasperating. My rises and falls in running embodied that of the "Thrill of Victory, Agony of Defeat" opener from TV's *Wide World of Sports*: the champion skier who in a split second found himself in the throes of a ghastly accident.

Then, for a magical period that spanned twenty-two months, the stars and heavenly bodies aligned. I locked in and rocked. I competed in seven marathons, twice notching the win.

In my one big race, in Boston, in a dream attempt to hit the Olympic Trials qualifying standard, I crashed during the second half of the dash to Beantown—but still wobbled home in 2:26:03. Count them, and in six of the seven 26.2-mile ventures in less than two years, I placed no worse than third. That's one very good run.

Glory, though, is relative. And excruciatingly fleeting. And timing and luck sometimes just don't line up. But no debating this: coming of age as a marathoner during the decade that kicked off a global sporting and lifestyle revolution was a thrilling and never replicated time to be a runner. The problem was everybody was good. While my Boston performance was laudable by the standards of any era, it gained me little. When I pinned on my competitor's number and legged myself from Hopkinton to Prudential Center, it earned me in 1981 a meaningless 165th. Nice try, kid, but no cash prize, free shoes, offer to move to Oregon to train with the big boys, or Olympic Trials. Just a standard finisher's medal and painful six-hour drive that night back to the PA hinterlands.

What I hadn't known then was I had peaked five months earlier when I clocked a faster time at Harrisburg. By Boston I was going the wrong way. After Beantown came a landslide of injuries and declining performances, with my last race worth mentioning, third in Atlantic City, at age thirty.

The cruel truth is, before twenty-five, I was past prime. By my early thirties, headed for oblivion; by fifty, sixty, and now sixty-eight, one doesn't need to know. But should anybody see a slow guy shuffling through the neighborhoods of Allentown, Pennsylvania, toot, that's probably me.

By 1999, at forty-three, I'd have my first of five major medical interventions to correct heart-rhythm abnormalities. Call it, generically, a-fib. And who knows what was going down inside my chest earlier.

Life is good. Then it evens out.

Maybe I should've stuck with the Appalachian Trail.

◊

As the running movement gained wider popularity with the emergence of the corporate-backed mega race, so diminished its earlier hippie composition. Before the sport's originals could utter holy Ronnie, our country's electorate had selected an anti-environmental president to the right of

Nixon; and those who forked over the race entry fees were as apt to be lawyers and traders in their day jobs as hanger-on students or substitute math teachers. It's the way life seemed to work. It swung from polestar to polestar. Carter to Reagan. Clinton to Bush. Obama to Trump. Backpacking in cutoffs and discount-store work boots to donning lab-tested synthetic wicking fabrics and sticker-shock-priced designer footwear.

After the second college, I went to work for three and a half decades in newspaper and magazine journalism, higher-ed public relations, coaching, teaching, writing and editing. I moved around some, even briefly back to New Jersey. By my middle twenties I had returned to PA, and without a master plan, seeded the ground and planted roots that inexorably grew deeper each year. That was mainly in Allentown. Where they've shut down the factories, closed the mills, and bet the future of the city on minor-league hockey. But it's okay, living here in Allentown.

Hiking, held at bay for three decades by running's feel-good effect on the brain and body, became a second choice for me. Although trails to walk continued to beckon and my desire to explore them never went cold. I got outside and about when hiking fit into the schedule. It became a time-gap-filler activity; more hobby, less a goal-driven pursuit. Not to mention an important exercise option when the wear and tear from the running became too much. Along the way, I logged some good hikes in good places.

In the years after 1970-73 and the Brugmann expeditions, I added pieces of new Appalachian Trail mileage in Pennsylvania, Maryland, and Massachusetts. And where routes walked during the seventies had been altered, I returned to inspect the new alignments. In Connecticut, New Jersey, New York. Numerous times I visited eastern PA's Pinnacle, the can't-miss overlook Bob, Jeb, and I managed to miss in '72. During the nineties I joined the ATC and have stayed a member. A couple of times for chuckles more than profundity, I've read Bill Bryson's acclaimed book, *A Walk in the Woods*, and other Appalachian Trail stories. Bryson's is fun reading, more fluff than substance, not to be taken too seriously. But I never turned down a good hiking book, such as *Wild* by Cheryl Strayed, or an opportunity to unfold a trail map and escape into it.

Twice or three times, I returned to Mount Mansfield. On each occasion I hoisted myself over its naked, wind-whipped Chin to the summit. What acrophobia and inexperience stopped me from doing at twelve, I could manage as a young adult without much trouble. To overcome a personal fear at any age feels rewarding.

Ignoring old fears, however, could be dangerous. In two tries, a pal from my dorm at Lyndon State and I managed to bobble over the Long Trail's northern dozen miles to the Canadian border. Not far from our campus, Vermont's best-known hiking route passed on its journey to Quebec. Within weeks of meeting Gerry, we had plotted a hike on the LT.

On our first attempt to reach the border I aborted the hike after what began as a stray October shower turned into an icy, hypothermia-inducing steady rain. Thankfully, I kept my head screwed on enough to get my slurry-speech companion off the mountaintop, warmed up and coherent, during an hours' long walk and hitch back to his car. As observed before, bad things out there tend to happen when you don't see them coming. We were working on a disaster, and my still-fresh memory of Bob's death on this same trail 170 miles to the south fifteen months before perhaps signaled the alarm to my brain soon after Gerry exhibited out of character agitation.

My biggest post-Brugmann hike of all was Katahdin in 2006, a month before my fiftieth birthday. I was talked into this madness by Fred Follansbee. A young Maine native and free spirit, Fred ran under my coaching tutelage at Muhlenberg College and went on to serve in the Peace Corps in Zambia. We became beer buddies. He knew my interest in hiking and reserved a campsite at Baxter State Park. Thankfully, Fred also invited along an experienced Mainer he knew, David White, who was my age.

In a few well-selected words in his 1973 postcard, Bob Brugmann said plenty when he compared New Hampshire's lunar-like White Mountains—"tough country," he called it—with Maine's 5,269-foot mass of granite. "Actually," Bob observed, "nothing [comes close] to Mt. Katahdin, which was great."

To reach the northern terminus of the AT to begin any official southbound hike, as was Bob's intention, the hiker first must conquer Katahdin. He could go up the severe-boulder-scramble AT route to the summit (known as the Hunt Trail), turn around, descend what was just climbed, then proceed à la General Sherman straight to Georgia. But no hiker wanted to repeat unnecessary miles—not when he has some 2,190 ahead. Most likely, Bob ascended Katahdin from the closest trailhead to Millinocket, the campground at Chimney Pond; same as Fred, David, and I did thirty-three years later.

I must agree with Bob's assessment of Katahdin being singularly great. Nothing I've hiked in fifty-five years of exploring on foot could compare to this giant, which translates to "main mountain" or "greatest mountain" in the Abenaki language. Formidable as New Hampshire's above-timberline skyscrapers were, mean as a single Adirondacks peak could be, Katahdin is on a different scale of ruggedness and steepness, accented with deadly drop-offs. It's the high end of hiking without crossing into climbing, which required ropes, harnesses, pitons, specialized training, and a recipe of courage beyond what I seemed to have.

I've been uncomfortable on some hikes. Those mentioned including Mount Mansfield, the Presidentials, the nastier ADKs; even briefly at Lehigh Gap and the Lemon Squeezer. But never, except on Katahdin, have I been as far out of my comfort zone for as many hours as I was on the ascent via the Cathedral Trail, and across the mile-long Knife Edge. Thank God for David's counsel in getting me up the mountain, across the vertiginous Knife Edge, and down the almost as precarious Dudley Trail back to the campground. Had I followed Fred's loosey-goosey climbing style, I might have fallen very far.

So what Bob called "great," I'd amend to borderline terrifying, intimidating, risky, and not for somebody who is jittery around heights. In regards to scale, the views, the wilderness setting, rough terrain, and near constant exposure, Bob was spot on: Katahdin's great. But would I go back? Only if somebody knew an easier route up. Otherwise, once was enough. I enjoyed the thrill—but not until I was back at the campground undamaged and able to admire the view from down there. It was certainly one of those adventures that are amazing when you look back at what you did, but suck while you're doing them. I've never claimed to be a superstar at this.

When Bob went up, he was just a boy scout-molded kid from New Jersey, a few days removed from school exams and teen life. Next thing he knew he's hanging on ledges inching up a huge mountain, hauling everything he needed to survive on his back, trying to calculate with each step the best placement strategy for his feet and fingers without losing balance. And this was just the introduction to his great adventure.

Katahdin's a wicked mountain. A single misstep can end it all. No wonder my friend had acquired some confidence by the time he reached feisty Clarendon Gorge a month later down the trail.

Part Seven

Family Business

36. Millie's Little Red House
West Barnet, Vermont; September 2021

The day after Jeb Brugmann's sixty-fourth birthday, we caught up at long last. Only weeks before I'd reached out to Millie to tell her about this book. She greenlighted my efforts and offered to work some back channels to bring her middle son and I together for an important reunion.

Millie's well into her ninth decade, retired from nursing and lives with two Border Collies in a red cottage that overlooks the Connecticut River valley. Jeb, with a canine companion of his own, was down from Toronto, able to leave Canada with the easing of Covid restrictions.

Despite being at HCHS together for a year after his brother's accident, I had only flashes of recollections of Jeb from that time. I was running by then, not hiking, and trying to parlay my middling GPA of Bs and Cs into a college acceptance—anywhere they'd take me. Save one post-high school conversation in a bar in Flemington (where he told me to afford college, he was living in a tent on the campus grounds), this was my first face-to-face since the Nixon administration with the surviving brother from our original hiking trio. After our return from New Hampshire a month after Bob's death, Jeb and I have lived a universe apart. It was nothing personal. Just the way the winds of life tossed us.

Jeb has mainly lived in Canada since 1991. When his travel schedule permits, he likes to compete in canoe marathons with his young-adult sons, Rashad and Kareem. He still manages the occasional wilderness backpacking trip.

As for Millie, she and I reconnected five years earlier, promised to keep in touch, had marginally done so, then lost additional time to Covid. The circumstances surrounding our 2016 reunion, however, were very important.

Aided by material gathered from online sleuthing, Jeb was as much as I expected him to be and how I remembered him: cordial, bespectacled, bald, lean and fit, introspective, scholarly—and prepared to talk about the past within some agreed upon limits. If I saw him on the streets of Toronto's Yorkville, Upper East Side Manhattan (where he'd once lived), or Johannesburg, I'd know him in an instant. Millie, a tiny, spunky woman who has weathered decades of anguish, was much sharper than she gave herself credit for. Together, mother and son patiently responded to four hours of sometimes nettlesome questions, sometimes remembering details differently, sometimes showing family contentiousness, sometimes in their voices and faces revealing the pain that persists.

Unquestionably, Bob's loss on July 4, 1973, remained a sad and unresolved day of ill fortune and despair for both. As Millie sighed, "We're still working on it."

It was my sense that Millie has lived long enough to accept to a degree that life, in its randomness, may take those who find themselves in the wrong place in overpowering circumstances. But when it's a son, this paragon of goodness, just starting out in the world…

sometimes anger flared and grief surfaced. More than once she told me the story of her being in Flemington after the accident and seeing a group of idle youths on the street with pot. "Why Bob, and not one of these kids? Why my son, who had so much to offer?"

The promise I saw in both brothers back then is reflected today in Jeb's work. Sifting through the jargon of his professional life to the best of my understanding, Jeb's specialty was the study of city metamorphosis in the age of globalization.

Working as a university-affiliated academic and worldwide consultant, Jeb examined the dynamics of mass migrations on the evolution of the twenty-first century megacity, primarily through the lenses of economics, but myriad other social, political, and environmental factors. This vast, almost bottomless, dense subject looks into what happened when newly arriving populations with unique needs, ambitions, and skill sets bump against each other and vie for a piece of the economic pie inside an existing urban order. To cite two examples:

Northern Indians, fleeing desertification of their traditional homeland, occupy vacant spaces surrounding Mumbai and metastasize the local food-market landscape. On a smaller scale, Somali war refugees by the hundreds resettle in Lewiston, Maine, and find and seize opportunity in local coffee-shop operations. Bad or good, what are the ripple effects in the community and greater city?

Jeb lays out his thoughts on the future of cities in his 2009 book, *Welcome to the Urban Revolution: How Cities Are Changing the World*.[24] It's an academic treatise best-suited for grad-level economic geography or urban studies, but with sticking power, informative and precise—Jeb Brugmann, scholar, at his finest. Throughout fifteen laser-

---

24   2009: Bloomsbury Press, New York

focused chapters my old trail mate tirelessly argues that much of the unrest in the world, going back to the early industrialization period, can be traced to mass human movement from rural to urban places—for what Jeb calls "urban advantage." That is, capitalistic opportunity inherent to urban-based systems of commerce: retail, food service, tech and telecommunications sales and support, etc.

Insofar I could glean from its 330 ink-dense pages, what's absent in Jeb's book is humor. But the topics the author covers, among them the Iranian revolution of 1978-79 that chased the shah into exile and foisted on the West the Ayatollah Khomeini, were no joking matter.

When we got to Bob and what career path he'd have taken, Millie spoke and teared up. "I don't know what he would've become, but I know he would've been great."

According to Jeb, Bob had notions of studying at what is today the SUNY College of Environmental Science and Forestry, which shared facilities and a cross-registration arrangement with Syracuse University. Once his brother figured out the academic side of forestry was as much about commercial tree harvesting as resource protection, Jeb speculated Bob would have shifted to environmental studies and later veered towards law and policy. Of course it's all, as is any conversation about Bob's future, an educated guess.

One of the bigger surprises to come out of our wandering talk was the apparent ease with which Bob and Jeb got the OK from Central to leave school early and return late from their 1973 hikes. Gone the first of June, back during September. No exact date, fellas; no worries, ma'am. Millie remembered writing a straightforward request letter, couching her sons' trips as "educational," and received an unconditional approval—with no required learning component such as journaling or tying their adventures to Bob's nascent environmental course. HCHS's leniency with the brothers' request was stunning. For sure, Bob and Jeb were scholastically sound and played by the rules. They had leverage with teachers and the administration. However, this was an era before it was common for every other parent to pull kids from classes for Disney, skiing, beach vacations, or cousin anybody's destination wedding. Was getting out of school always this easy? What Millie pulled off my old-school parents would never dared try.

By prior arrangement with Jeb, we agreed to circumvent any discussion about the brothers' decisions to split up and go solo in '73 and its safety implications. Nonetheless, from my own hiking experiences and knowledge of the accident, I offer my own take.

Whether due exclusively to the messy circumstances that marred their aborted 1972 New England hike or the surfacing of individual goals and independent streaks, Bob and Jeb set a precedent when they separated in Vermont, and a second time that same summer in New Jersey; to hike where, when, how, and with whom they wished. Despite their tender ages, both brothers, I've always maintained, were fully capable backpackers. They were also self-reliant doers whose social needs were secondary to the tasks at hand. Rather than risk a repeat rise in tension that surfaced on the trail the year before, it was logical to think that with longer hikes to tackle in '73, each brother concluded he (and, by extension, they) would be better off to go alone and keep fraternal disagreements at rest.

As I saw it, they were sufficiently safe doing so. Despite its lower usage then, there was an increasing presence of long-distance hikers on the AT, as Bob had assured our schoolmate Dennis Shuman. If you wanted a buddy for 100 or 250 miles for safety or someone to talk to, your chances of finding a companion were good. The brothers' plan—of Bob starting from Maine, Jeb from Georgia, and meeting in the middle before continuing their respective journeys—few would argue against it being a nifty idea. It was something the Brugmanns would think of doing and be resourceful enough to execute.

Upon reading literature on outdoor safety, authoritative sources uniformly discouraged solo hiking. This was reasonable, but the on-the-ground reality for many who inhabited trails was different. By their nature, hikers were individualists who valued solitude and didn't easily integrate with others' walking speeds or social peccadillos. Many were comfortable risking the remote chance of a mishap while alone for the mental nourishment and solitude of moving through the woods at his own pace, with his own thoughts. Talk little, think deep; take pictures, pee breaks, and lunch stops—or no stops at all—at our discretion. I would fall into this camp, as did Bob and Jeb.

Jeb made this clear: the summer of '73 was not supposed to be some single-season thru-hike attempt. Each brother would cover as much trail as he could in his three-to-four-month June into September window, then finish up what he didn't get to do the next year. Jeb also dismissed anything I speculated earlier about Bob or him passing up previously hiked AT sections—Bear Mountain to the Susquehanna River and possibly other parts, to expedite their walks. "We were doing the whole thing," he told me. No cutting corners, no liberties with mileage covered on earlier hikes. In the eyes of the ATC and demigod of the thru-hike, Ed Garvey, any accomplishment short of every mile didn't count. Bob and Jeb wanted to count. And scouts' honor, this pair of brothers, together or apart, would never cheat or fudge a thing.

No matter, Bob's aggressive hiking across the tough miles of Maine and New Hampshire as we learned from an old trail companion had raised questions about personal factors that might've influenced Bob's thinking when he reached Clarendon Gorge. From trying to satisfy goals that differed from Jeb's, to combating loneliness, to feeling frustrated by his slowed-down progress, to mulling thoughts about suspending the hike two days hence at Manchester. Besides his heavy pack, what was weighing the kid down when he arrived at VT 103?

On June 2, 1973, Jeb flew to Atlanta and by combination of bus and his thumb, reached the approach trail to the Appalachian Trail in far northern Georgia and began hiking that same day. Two or three days later, Bob disembarked from a bus in the Maine mill town of Millinocket, the gateway to Baxter State Park: home of Katahdin and the northern terminus of the great AT.

◊

When I ventured to ask him about his two years at HCHS after Bob's accident, Jeb responded to my inquiry with a couple of facial twitches and few words. From what I could gather: he was in a miasma of withdrawal, if relieved some by his urge to satisfy incomplete hiking goals. Jeb returned to the AT in the spring of '74, picked up the pathway near the Potomac River, and walked the remaining parcels he needed into Pennsylvania. Late that summer, he jumped back on the trail in the White Mountains and finished out the behemoth to Katahdin.

In a patchwork of section hiking over a period of three years, 1972 to 1974, Jeb could claim and would be recognized as an Appalachian Trail end-to-end traveler—not a coveted thru-hiker, who must complete the distance within a year's time. Regardless of organizational specifications, two weeks before he turned seventeen, Jeb had bagged a full AT.

In the years ahead he'd shift from HCHS to Hamilton College and landed seasonal employment with the Green

Mountain Club as caretaker of its Long Trail camp facilities at Stratton Pond and Cooper Lodge. Both of which were pivotal stops in Bob's journeys up and down the trail. During his GMC tenure, Jeb tallied at least one hike of the entire Long Trail.

Hamilton is a highly selective liberal arts school in Clinton, New York, near Utica. Its alumni include thinkers such as Ezra Pound and B.F. Skinner while Alex Haley and Bernie Sanders had taught there. Jeb entered as a philosophy major where he seemed a good fit. Except after a year of study abroad in Germany, he left Hamilton. Perhaps it was the school's patriarchal bent—strong teams in basketball, hockey, and lacrosse—that soured him; or that the place had yet to fully open its doors to women; or just the prohibitive cost. To afford Hamilton, Jeb tent-camped on college property until driven inside school buildings during the most frigid of nights. He was this outlier on a campus full of fraternities and boarding-school money; a kid who washed dishes in high school to stash away dollars for college. In the end, Jeb would transfer and finish his undergraduate studies in economics at UMass in Amherst.

Millie parted with her beloved horses, bought a different style of boot, and hit the trails. "I wanted to see what Bob and Jeb liked about hiking. I was an equestrienne, and never thought I'd hike." She eventually covered the Long Trail in sections, accompanied by a favorite black Lab, Ellie. Millie also returned to the classroom and transitioned from corporate middle management to nursing by the age of forty-five.

Inspired by her deceased son's totality of commitment to his causes, Millie said she became "determined to make humanity better in some way that I could. For me, that was giving up pretty good pay to become a critical-care nurse." In 1990, she also said goodbye to New Jersey for Vermont. "Knowing how much Bob loved it here, being here feels right." She did leave for a dozen years to be near grandchildren in the Midwest but returned to Vermont by 2015 and became, with an assist from the Border Collies she trained, a sheepherder.

Jeb's migration through young adulthood would incrementally pull him away from mountain summits and ridgelines into cities teeming with people, culture, universities, and ideas. And into the maw of the larger question of economic and environmental accommodation for growing urban populations against the forces of strained natural resources, inequity, unfriendly politics, and climate change. The author bio on his book's dustjacket summarized him as a "strategy consultant to organizations and leaders internationally" who takes on "global issues at the local level." It further cited Jeb as "founding secretary general" of an agency with global reach: the International Council for Local Environmental Initiatives. Think urban sustainability with a focus on entrepreneurial opportunity for the poor in the age of globalization.

Jeb's unquestionably a well-connected, global-reaching professional. But while responding to my questions, he was hand-cranking apples fallen from his mother's trees to make applesauce in her tiny kitchen. Hyperlocal sustainability in action.

Jeb's first urban-centric living experience can be traced to his year abroad at age 21 in Freiburg, southwest Germany, which counts about 700,000 people in its metropolitan area. Later, as a Harvard grad student, he joined a Greater Boston community of more than three million.

Jeb dedicated his book to a former colleague and, of course, his late brother, for being his "mentors in life and in the cause of sustainable development." The formal tribute to

Bob was endearing and the part about Bob as a mentor to Jeb remained appropriate and true. However, any inference in the text (if read verbatim) that Bob was a key influence in making urban sustainability his career could, in my opinion, be misleading. Unless he worked in a big law firm or high up in government, had Bob lived, I believed his temperament and talents were better suited to wilderness preservation, or science or policy-based work in support of land conservation. Anything smacking of urban, say inside I-287 in New Jersey, tended to bum Bob out.

I asked Jeb what was Bob's biggest influence on him: What quality about himself can he most attribute to his deceased brother? "His leadership initiative," Jeb told me. "When Bob launched the township recycling program or developed the curriculum for the environmental course at school, he inspired me to become an initiator."

Indeed, Bob was seemingly born to be in charge. Five and a half decades ago our gym teacher saw this ability and selected him to captain a seventh-grade basketball team. At fourteen he led his brothers and father down an Adirondack peak in dangerous weather. At sixteen he influenced the school administration to see the forest through the trees and (rather counterintuitively) legalized student smoking. And, no contest, he was the top dishwasher at Fiddler's Inn. Bob wasn't loud nor did he exhibit a hint of swagger, but he was steadfast in his actions. A leader you could count on.

Jeb's master's degree was in public administration from Harvard's John F. Kennedy School of Government. He's also completed coursework at Harvard Business School and has published in the Harvard Business Review. Jeb has worked in twenty-eight countries and served as a senior associate on the faculty at the University of Cambridge in the U.K.

37. Paul Brugmann
Columbia, Missouri

Millie's third son was born in Michigan on June 15, 1959, making him three years younger than Bob and Jeb's baby brother by twenty-one months. In school placement, when the family arrived in Readington, Bob would enter fifth grade, Jeb fourth, Paul second. When Bob began high school in 1970, Paul would start sixth grade. Paul had just turned eleven when Bob led his father and two brothers down a precipitous, rain-slickened path from giant Algonquin Mountain to the refuge of a shelter. It was, for the child, a traumatic experience. "It had started out a nice day, and then the weather turned bad," recalled Paul. "My sleeping bag was soaked, and I sensed fear on my dad's part."

Paul was a mere shaver when I knew him. A barely-there nearly wordless child on those occasions I could remember him inside the house on Hillcrest Road, or in the car with his brothers, Millie, or Mike. Today he's a new grandad at age sixty-five, father of three young adults, and husband to Monica. After college, Paul and Monica settled in the U.S. heartland in central Missouri. As Bob and Jeb were the family leaders in hiking, environmental activism, and scholastic achievement, young Paul was at a disadvantage to vie for attention and accolades against this pair of "superstar" older brothers, as Jeb unabashedly referred to himself and Bob.

"So," as Jeb told me, "Paul anchored his identity in other ways... anything with wheels and an engine." Or as Millie put it, "Paul suffered from being the third brother, the odd man out, and to survive turned to cars and motorcycles."

Paul didn't disagree. "Bob and Jeb had a strong alliance at any early age." Instead of gravitating as his older siblings had to band, sports, scout-troop projects, or student government, the youngster connected with a local stock-car driver and found sources of income doing chores on nearby farms afterschool and weekends. Paul also remembered growing up in a less than idyllic home environment of tight finances and strife associated with some of the men in Millie's life.

When Millie's and Mr. Brugmann's marriage dissolved, the brothers with their mother returned to New Jersey to a location close to her parents. This was Pluckemin, a village at the intersection of middle-class Bridgewater Township and country clubby Bedminster, in Somerset County, where the family rented for three years. Nearby were Mr. and Mrs. George Nutz, the grandparents, who resided in a home ascended from a small lakeside resort.[25]

Times here, as Paul hasn't forgotten, were tense. While Millie collected a decent-size paycheck from her work in HR at Colgate-Palmolive, a remarriage to a volatile ex-marine who managed a service station was poisonous. "He

---

[25] This is Sunset Lake. Despite encroachments from I-287 and I-78, the community retains a tourist-camp feel suggestive of a 1920s resort, with a swimming beach, fresh water for fishing and paddling, and a woodsy Watchung Mountains setting, maintained by a residents' association. Jeb credits his grandfather's role in the lake's upkeep for helping ignite his and Bob's interests in natural resources protection.

was abusive to Bob," Paul remembered. "He was angry about something, and Bob gave him this look of defiance or skepticism and was beaten."

After the move to the rancher in Readington in '66—with according to Paul "a significant amount of financial help" from the Nutzes—came more stability, though it was not a utopia. By now Millie and the abusive second husband had parted. A more likable boyfriend arrived, the kids settled in new schools and routines, and there was space for Millie's horses. But with Mike being younger than Millie by several years and occupying part of the living room, the youngest Brugmann son recalled the visitor's presence feeling like "the older stepbrother who returns home after being away than a father figure we could look up to." The siblings' arrangement with W. James Brugmann: one weekend a month with visitations divided between New York City (where he lived) and northern New Jersey (the home of his parents). This worked okay until high school. By then, as Bob's and Jeb's interests in backpacking, school activities, and earning money took precedent over the scheduled weekends with dad, ties with their father weren't as strong, and Mr. Brugmann's unlikely transformation from auto-industry adman into an urban minister took shape. "Dad was in our lives, but we didn't see a lot of him," Paul recalled.

Amidst this tumult of divorces, moves, financial insecurity, awkwardness with houseguests, and a father who would come out as gay, Bob was a beam of light. "His compass," as Paul remembered, "was intrinsically set on true north." Meaning—Bob saw through the complexity of life and came out of every crisis and imbroglio tougher and stronger.

But as the third-wheel little brother, Paul found Bob's ideals smothering. "I gave up on trying to live up to his and Jeb's standards and by eighth grade got into drugs." Regrettably, Paul remembered being on the outs with his oldest sibling in

'73 when he left for Maine. "Bob tried to be the man of the house, which I rejected. We were on bad terms."

Paul vividly recalled the evening at Hillcrest when the phone call came. "We were cooking hamburgers and hot dogs on the Fourth of July." Paul believed it was his mom, not Mike, who answered, and who leaned against a wall in disbelief, gathering sketchy information from the Vermont State Police. The rest that followed—frantic packing, a nighttime drive to Rutland, days of searching for his missing brother—for Paul was like being lost inside a fogbank. Then, following cremation, services for Bob in Stanton and Mr. Brugmann's chapel in Jersey City, he would stumble into high school and wobble to the end. He got by from smoking weed, barely passing classes, finding low-pay work, and surviving clashes with school authority. Unlike his brothers, Paul said he had "no aspirations of going to college." He and Jeb attended HCHS together for two years but in any normal brotherly sense were seas apart.

"Jeb was an odd bird in high school," as Paul remembered, and one could see what Paul meant in the yearbook photos. Jeb in his few appearances in *The Echo* does a good John Lennon impersonation as a shades-wearing bohemian and is conspicuously missing from the senior portrait section. No photo, no bio, no record of Jeb doing anything. Paul's own cameos are limited to a few homeroom group shots: a sneering kid, no trace of joy.

As much as a yearbook could be trusted, the post-accident Jeb seemed absorbed in faraway thoughts and a total rejection of traditional high school social conventions. Paul was the rogue who wasted the four years challenging rules and serving out detentions and suspensions.

Was Bob's misfortune at Clarendon Gorge the cause for both his brothers' teenage drift? Is global warming real?

Doing nothing better at nineteen than bouncing around

with buddies and working marginal jobs, Paul joined the Army and served for seven years. California. Germany. Savannah, Georgia. Guantanamo Bay. Honduras. A specialist in Cold War-era concerns, Paul's tasks included the monitoring of nuclear threats, watching for global communism expansion, and eyeing terrorist activity. Along the way he gained some confidence and found a direction in the Bible. "I kept bumping into people who talked about the Bible… it made sense and put things in order for me."

Paul was twenty-six, back with Millie in New Jersey, and going to community college when he met Monica at church. They clicked and would U-Haul themselves to Kansas where they continued their educations at MidAmerica Nazarene, a small evangelical college. Paul later earned a master's degree in sustainable agriculture from the University of Missouri. His career ranged from various sales endeavors to lab technologist. Today he's an avid cyclist and enjoys getting outside in nature much as his brothers did. Monica serves as a nurse in the local VA. Their three children have scattered—to Arkansas, Los Angeles, and Washington, D.C.

In some respects the two surviving brothers, Paul and Jeb, are as separated today as they were while roaming the hallways at HCHS post-accident. One is a Canadian-American academic with a global outlook and international influence living in a multicultural neighborhood in a left-leaning city in Canada. The other is a devout Christian, conservative, military vet residing in a deep red state. They live almost 900 miles apart and rarely see each other. As Paul saw it: "I gravitate towards conventional thinking, Jeb gravitates towards the unconventional. He's deeply philosophical and introspective. It makes us very different people and brothers."

Political, religious outlooks, and other divergent opinions

aside, they succeeded in caring for each other and peacefully coexist. "There is the sense that we're the ones [from the original three] left, which created a resolve that we need to put differences aside and have a healthy, brotherly understanding. We have a strong mutual respect for each other and walk away from the table at holidays without any negative feelings."

38. Anna Brugmann & Rashad Brugmann
District of Columbia and Vancouver, British Columbia

Anna Brugmann and Rashad Brugmann are cousins. Anna is Paul and Monica's middle child and oldest of two daughters. Rashad is the eldest of Jeb's two sons. Anna was born twenty years after Bob's death. Rashad is four years younger than her. When I reached out to both with nothing more than an introductory email to ask if they would talk about themselves and what they knew about Uncle Bob, both replied enthusiastically.

Anna lives in the District of Columbia and works for a nonprofit advocacy group for struggling newspapers called Rebuild Local News. She trained as a journalist at the University of Missouri, spent two years in Albania in the Peace Corps, and has worked for several news publications. She described herself as a hiker and urban explorer but hesitated to compare herself to Bob or Jeb.

"I knew only a little about Uncle Bob—that he and Uncle Jeb were starting at the far ends of the trail and were supposed to rendezvous somewhere in the middle," said Anna. "Sometime after they started there was a flash flood and it drowned Uncle Bob.

"But honestly, we didn't talk about what happened that much. I think it was a very painful topic for my father, Uncle Jeb, and Grandma Millie. Or maybe I was just caught up in my own growing up things and didn't pay a lot of attention to this older uncle I never knew." Anna did say that her father kept a photo of Bob's headstone over his dresser at home.[26]

Rashad trained as a civil engineer at the University of Toronto. He works in Vancouver as a building engineer for RDH, one of North America's leading firms in the design of energy efficient and sustainable structures. During his student years, on school vacations he served as a canoe guide for youth campers in northern Ontario. Paddling is Rashad's first love of multiple outdoor pursuits: backpacking, rock climbing, and backcountry ski touring among them. Even today, he'll commit work vacations to instructing young paddlers.

Rashad and his younger brother, Kareem, were raised in what Rashad described as "middle-class Toronto," with an Anglo father and Guyanese-Indian mother, in a multiethnic, cultural environment enhanced with books and ideas. But it was Jeb's interests and background of finding his modus operandi in the outdoors and getting a lot out of life on little money or material assets that most strongly influenced the boy. When the young man finished high school and elected to take a gap year before he began university studies, he stuck around home and worked as a construction laborer. As Rashad explained, "Thanks to having academic parents I grew up with some privilege for which I'm most grateful and went to an academically

---

[26] Following cremation, Bob's remains were placed in a location along the Appalachian Trail/Long Trail that is marked by a stone and cross. In respect to family privacy, I've not asked where this is.

enriched high school. But I felt my roots were blue-collar. Dad told me how he had to earn his way through school—by framing houses on a building crew, washing dishes, working on a chicken farm, and how he built a backpack from pieces of wood and some fabric he stitched together. I wanted to learn and experience that side of life."

The young man fondly recalled as a teenager teaming up with Jeb, Uncle Paul, and Paul's son Danny in a seventy-two-hour canoe race from Kansas City to St. Louis on the Missouri River. "But what I didn't appreciate at the time both in Missouri and on other expeditions was the anxiety my being on the water caused my father. This would stem from Uncle Bob's accident and my father's struggles with what happened. My dad's had to do a lot of internal work to get out of a depressive state, and his canoeing and eventual acceptance of my own whitewater trips, I think, has helped.

"Growing up, I saw that my dad and I had a lot in common," Rashad continued, "and I wanted to be like him. We especially connected through outdoor activities and with us both prioritizing having a positive impact on the world—socially, environmentally, anyway we could."

Neither Rashad nor Anna had visited their uncle's accident site in Vermont. Instead, the whims of life took them to other places, much the same as it dispersed the surviving Brugmann brothers from New Jersey to Ontario and Missouri. But Anna was ebullient in talking about how she cherishes her few opportunities to get together with her brother, sister, and their extended family in Canada. "Rashad, Kareem, Libby, Danny, and I have an altogether different relationship as cousins and siblings than I think Paul and Jeb, their wives, and Millie have had. Of course, they were more immediately impacted by what happened to Uncle Bob than us. But since we're all made from the same stuff, on some level I think everybody in the family is affected."

Part Eight

Back to the Garden (State)

39. Nowhereland
Readington, Flemington, Whitehouse Station; 1965-75

With Bob's accident half a century ago, his family long departed New Jersey, and many Lobbs gone as well, one triple-prong question keeps dragging me back to the old base camp. Where, and what exactly, was home for Bob, Jeb, and me in that amorphous midstate heath known as Readington? After a life away, why should this place matter enough to go back to hunt for clues and answers?

It matters because of how little it meant to us. We were three kids who grew up among these woods, declining farms, and rising subdivisions—without an identity we could easily inhabit or much hometown pride to infuse us. We intuitively knew that after high school we were going away, and not coming back. Why was that? Why did Jeb, Millie, and me and my brother all leave an area many considered attractive for economic advantage and desirability in raising families? And almost certainly, Bob would have exited too.

First consider us, the Lobbs. We were living in the sticks miles from anyplace in a new house on a newly paved cul-de-sac. Though assigned a Whitehouse Station address, we resided closest to Stanton with its village store and charming community church and hoped to fit in but seemed to lack the necessary pedigree. And my parents, almost pathologically modest people, would never schmooze their way into a place they knew they didn't belong. So there was no family claim to Stanton as home. No place for us either in the deeply Polish and Italian enclave of Whitehouse Station.

With Millie and her horses, the Brugmann boys landed in the barrens midway between Flemington, Whitehouse Station, and Somerville, a veritable middle of nowhere without a direct tie to any of those larger places. We were all, it seemed, doing time in this purgatory, awaiting college and its anticipated departure to anywhere but this jerseyography[27] of collapsing barns, scrub cedar, and thorny bushes.

Other factors that fed our feeling of disenfranchisement:

- **We were nonnatives to the area, outsiders through and through.** Seen by locals as having wealth, but existing paycheck-to-paycheck in heavily mortgaged homes.

- **Going to college meant going away, probably permanently.** The nearby schools that might accept us were in Trenton and New Brunswick—and no way we saw ourselves doing four years in either of those Jersey locations. With little thought I decamped to Vermont, Jeb to upstate New York, Ken to Michigan.

- **Whatever the career opportunities close to home were, corporate, teaching, family business, etc., we paid them no attention.** We wanted out.

---

27   Landforms, cultural, or development features common to New Jersey or popular perceptions and misperceptions of New Jersey (author's word and definition).

- **With its limited outdoor draw, the area never put hooks into us.** Except for Cushetunk Mountain[28] and Round Valley Reservoir, the Readington we knew was a void for the hiking and exploring we sought.

- **ZIP codes were meaningless.** Our respective Whitehouse Station and Flemington addresses connected us to neither town. We were fully decentralized.

- **With a 160-square-mile district and sprawling campus, going to HCHS felt more like a community college of hourly changing faces than having membership in a school of kids from a shared background.**

When people would ask, where you guys from, what would we say? Flemington, where we went to school? Whitehouse Station, where we bought groceries and played Little League but didn't fit in with the natives? Or Readington, where we paid the local tax but had no emotional investment or roots? It was a struggle to define "home" without an explanation. We would reply "outside of Whitehouse Station," "near Somerville," or "thirty miles north of Trenton." And leave it at that.

A good example of local identity confusion was Whitehouse Station. The town center included a bustling main street, a distinctive working-class culture, a station and train to New York. It was our commercial and residential hub. Yet Whitehouse Station had no self-government, police or municipal services of its own, or defined boundaries. It was all containerized inside Readington Township. Call it the biggest little town in

---

28   The Cushetunk ridgeline tops out at 837 feet, with sub-peak Round Mountain rising to 610 feet. This is not big sky country, but impressive in scale compared to the flat Jersey midlands to the east.

Hunterdon County that wasn't a town.

Superimposed on a map, Readington's shape approximated that of a turned around left hand. Within its forty-eight-square-mile mass sat a scattering of small communities, with Whitehouse Station at 3,500 the largest. Three Bridges, Stanton, Whitehouse, and Readington village also entered our story. The Brugmanns were positioned in eastern Readington Township; our family was in the northwest. House to house was five miles. Others we knew in the township might be eight or nine miles from their best pal, which by our state's dense population standards might well be Perth Amboy. Without help from a parent or a good bicycle, to see a school friend from Stanton Station, Centerville, or East Whitehouse was rare. At HCHS, distances were greater. A girl I wanted to date lived alongside the Delaware River across from Pennsylvania. Door to door, that's twenty-one miles. So drop that thought.

The township congealed into a single entity upon reaching high school; we became a "sending district." But wherever we were, Bob, Jeb, Ken and I and no doubt many others in our class of outsiders felt a bit lost in this space and place and sort of knew it. There was little to come back to. We were estranged from our hometown, this Nowhereland of New Jersey.

40. Changes
Hunterdon County, New Jersey

Could a 1970s story about three "regular" teenage boys who bonded on the Appalachian Trail, and one dies, gain traction in today's eclectic publishing landscape? Without getting into the stickiness of race, diversity, gender, segregation? More directly: Could this straight white male, 68, creditably wax in the syrup of DEI, LGBTQ+, or BIPOC?

No. So he wouldn't... but a little.

Truth be said, the AT the Brugmanns and I hiked, and the scouting system that shaped Bob and Jeb into proficient young backpackers, was about as Caucasian as a yacht club regatta. Color, as it rubbed against our lives and was missing from our trails, won't be deeply addressed. Other than to say we probably didn't think about it. We were kids who played in the woods. Period.

We stuck with what we knew: the AT, the state's northwest milk counties, and our all-white yellow school buses, classrooms, churches, cul-de-sacs, grocery stores, and everything else. Newark, New Brunswick, East Orange, Trenton, Paterson, and Plainfield were those other parts of

Jersey we did our best to ignore.

But if I could dedicate an anthem to Bob and Jeb, it would be "If I Had a Hammer." Written by Pete Seeger and recorded most famously by Peter, Paul, and Mary, the song starts out forebodingly, warning of dangers throughout the land. By the final stanza, a more hopeful message prevails; that being of unconditional love. Love that superseded political boundaries, or race, religion, and identity.

We called it being prejudiced: stereotyping based on color, ethnicity, accent, language, or religion. My impression is Bob and Jeb were two of the least prejudiced and most noncombative, nonjudgmental souls alive. Same as they were super hikers, high scholastic achievers, and bigger than their age thinkers, they were ahead of the curve in understanding the complexities of human rights and discrimination.

Looking back, our time at HCHS was a wildly contradictory period of optimism in race—listen to our songs!—amidst an entrenched bigotry that cloaked county farms, ranch homes, and the new colonials my father and Uncle Gene built and sold. But in the anomaly our school was, I remember it being a safe space for our tiny minority population. There was denigrating locker-room banter couched as "humor" and the occasional N-word heard. Yet the hallway environment seemed closer to love than to disrespect or something worse. If one excelled in something, sports, academics, music, no matter their skin color or ethnicity they were protected by friends and teammates. Their passage through was okay.

The Hunterdon County we relocated to in the 1960s was starch-white with micro communities of color in Flemington and Lambertville. When the state from Paterson to Newark, Plainfield to New Brunswick, and Asbury Park to Atlantic City, boiled over in violence, a building boom here followed, fed by resettlement from towns to the east.

This was the migration known as white flight; and coming from Fanwood (next to minority-majority Plainfield), we were undeniably part of it. In the municipal governments our parents and neighbors would elect, de facto segregation measures sculpted as good policy were passed. To strengthen a building code without appearing too discriminatory.

My sentiments about the old county and how it has grown are warm, generally. The conservationist inside my psyche applauded the proactive stand Hunterdon had undertaken to save many thousands of acres of farmland, waterways, woods, and hillsides from landscape-altering and ecologically destructive development. The small-town charm has been preserved. Except for the major road corridors, sprawl around Flemington, and some clusters of McMansions, the county has hung on to a look that's not unrecognizably changed from what I recalled. As one with a long memory and nostalgic yen, I find this comforting.

But one reason it looks like it does could be traced to factors beyond a conservation ethic. For decades the building codes have been written in ways that open doors to the affluent and close them to the less affluent. It's called exclusionary zoning. EZ works two ways. By requiring a residential property to meet a minimum size requirement (say, five acres) before the town will issue a building permit, the official thinking is you limit growth while adding dollars to your tax base, "save" open space, and to a degree keep your rural appearance. Of course, nobody but the well-off can afford to occupy a triple-garage-door home starting at half a million on an old cornfield lot in Readington.

Is EZ a prime example of structural racism—or a proactive measure to stanch sprawl, preserve green spaces, and retain a look that's considered desirable? In my head I asked the Brugmanns. Jeb, an urban globalist, would likely see it as policy driven by race. Bob would agree with Jeb but might concede that the preservation effort of the past half century had been beneficial to local biodiversity and a key to opening environmentally compatible recreation opportunities and forms of tourism anchored in farm products and viticulture.

What about change on the Appalachian Trail in fifty years and in organizations like the Appalachian Trail Conservancy and Appalachian Mountain Club whose membership fees sustained it? In a nod to this great footpath, in fifty-four years of hiking in thirteen states I've yet to encounter a sign denying any racial or cultural group access. Yet its use remains largely white. The ATC, AMC, and Green Mountain Club have come to see the value and moral responsibility of bringing underrepresented populations to their pathways. They've committed resources to correct past practices that were less welcoming to folks beyond their historic base and talk about equity and diversity in their bylaws, publications, and operations. But progress in such matters, as measured by who one sees using the trails, has been slow.

In the county where Bob, Jeb, and I found common ground, in drops and dribbles more nonwhite individuals and families have filtered into HCHS and other schools and towns. Communities are inching in directions that look more like modern America.[29] On the trails, if grindingly slow, DEI, LGBTQ+, and BIPOC is making gains.

Bob understood how organizational systems worked, and how to bring change to them without overturning the apple cart and sparking a donnybrook. He would cheer the progress. Jeb would see the progress too—albeit more skeptically: with a limp thumbs' up and wary eye. *As brothers they were similar, yet different.*

---

[29] New population groups are arriving in Hunterdon more rapidly than in the past. A HCHS faculty member told me in his nine years at the school, the identified white enrollment has fallen from eighty-eight to seventy-five percent.

41. Trail Town

Readington and Northwestern New Jersey; 2024

If Bob was visiting Readington, I'd suggest a hike. Meet near his old house and enter the fields at the Hillcrest Road trailhead. Continue across them to Cole Road and beyond it to 523. Next cross Stanton Ridge, where we'd comment less than kindly on its mini-Mar-a-Lago bearing and wide paved walking path that appeared to get no use.[30] Then re-enter the trails network at the Bouman-Stickney farmstead on Dreahook Road and spend a few hours exploring a variety of fields, Round Mountain, and riverine lowlands. Returning, we'd select other trails to get across the mountain; and I'd suggest a stop at the 1840 vintage Stanton General Store for a bite of its Mexican fare. Finally, after a second hustle across the golf course, we could retrace the trails back to Hillcrest, or break for a beer at Nancy's house near Cole Road. Total distance, around twenty miles; fifteen or so of them on trails. Another time, we would

---

30 The property cited in "Scout & Wander Boy" that stood as my play paradise into my early teens. Once open fields, it now hosts fairways and seven-figures housing. The view of Cushetunk Mountain dead ahead is still nice.

tackle as many as sixteen miles at Round Valley Reservoir via its own trail system.

Bob would enjoy this.

Since the time our families arrived there, the middle sixties, Readington's population tripled to almost 20,000. What's also dramatically changed is marked trails everywhere enable most anyone with two feet and a wander gene or a saddle to get happily lost inside this rusticated suburb. Who could have imagined it? When Bob, Jeb, and I were teens, local hiking was limited to the new Round Valley trail. Or if you had my yearnings, by following the farm lanes and woods roads, one could improvise through stealth and bushwacking a hike to most anywhere. Follow the old tracks and trust the landowners to be tolerant of trespassing kids, as most were.

Readington today identifies twenty properties with public access for hiking and horses. Add some sites just beyond the borders, and the list expands to twenty-five locations. At Cushetunk Mountain, my old stamping grounds, state, county, and township-built trails connect much of the mountain. Between Stanton and the Raritan River, including Round Mountain, lies a wide-ranging system anchored by Deer Path Park. Another cluster of marked routes has opened on idle agricultural lands between Hillcrest Road and Cole Road, a short walk from the Lobb family home in the township and current residence of Nancy Lobb. None of this was here fifty years ago.

What happened to turn this rather ordinary spread of mid-state fields and patchy woods in the eye of developers into a model for limited growth, land and farm preservation, and future outdoor recreation opportunities? What's more fun to talk about than the debatable motives of EZ is township voters, in 1978, approved the state's first open-space ballot referendum. Its long-term outcome has kept a third of Readington under protection as farm and conservation lands. As properties enrolled in the program, a secondary "greenways" initiative spurred the creation of public trails on these lands. Today the township can boast 9,000 acres of preserved open space and a mile of trail for every 2.4 square miles of land.

The system is not flawless. Maintenance can fall on efforts of volunteer labor; and seasonal overgrowth and fear of tick-borne illnesses can be an impediment to use. Trail activity is medium. A link in the system that would connect Round Mountain with Cushetunk Mountain is missing. But what's established is good. If not yet a magnet for active recreation, that potential exists. People with vision and voters willing to fund a progressive idea have in their backyards places to hike that weren't conceivable to Jeb, Bob, or me in the 1970s.

An hour away, other protections have brought benefits to the Appalachian Trail through the northwest of the Garden State. The forty-mile Water Gap-to-High Point section we knew as kids is improved with the establishment of the National Recreation Area and (painful as it was) removal of communities of people. Swinging east, five decades ago the AT from High Point was a road walk across wide valleys of mixed subdivisions and farmland—nobody's idea of a good hike. Today's route includes a mile-long boardwalk crossing of the Pochuck swamp, passage through the Wallkill River National Wildlife Refuge flatlands, and a nice NPS corridor inside woodlands. Then back to the rugged terrain of Wawayanda State Park before the pathway slides north into New York.

Amid a dimmer outlook on climate and other environmental threats—the same worries times a half century of firmer scientific evidence; debate, inaction, and stalling; and an urgency that moved the Brugmanns and

I into becoming young ecology crusaders—it's a comfort to have good news of any kind to talk about. Readington's land-saving measures and various protections precipitated by the routing of the AT demonstrate what's achievable in environmental security when people, elected officials, funding, and laws work in unison. Amen!

Part Nine

Reconstruction

42. Clarendon Gorge
Green Mountain National Forest, Vermont

Thanks to membership support, state resources, and $1,300 culled from the friends and family of Bob Brugmann—including the remaining $370 of dimes and quarters from Bob's own savings account, donated posthumously by Millie—the Green Mountain Club was able to spearhead an engineering and construction miracle and reopen a new bridge at the gorge less than fourteen months after Bob's fall. Worksite building activity to official opening took but three months. It was a reminder of what's possible when people from the hiking community come together, hire local talent, put to work a few college kids, engage skilled volunteers, apply some Vermonter ingenuity, and give them the resources and materials they need to get a job done—quickly, efficiently, and within a budget.

The Bob Brugmann Footbridge opened in late August 1974, replacing the 1958 suspension bridge taken out by the Mill River flood of June 30, 1973. The "new" bridge underwent major repairs in 2008 and 2021 and remains one of the most important pieces of infrastructure along the 272-mile Long Trail. Although it sways as a suspension bridge should, the bridge was solidly built, and fulfilled its purpose as a safe crossing of the Mill in ways both functional and aesthetically pleasing. It's a substantial structure, if miniaturized by the greater landscape of the surrounding geology. From the bottom of the gorge a visitor must scan the horizon and almost squint to locate the span.

According to *The Long Trail News*, the newsletter of the Green Mountain Club, reconstruction costs alone for the GMC in 1974 were in the vicinity of $8,000. Gifts from family sources "contributed substantially" to the project's financial bottom line. Recalibrated to modern inflation-adjusted rates, the total cost for the GMC to replace the bridge was around $48,000.

The club estimated one-hundred people attended the bridge dedication. Millie performed a ceremonial ribbon cutting. The Rev. W. James Brugmann offered the Lord's Prayer and words to the effect that Bob's "church" was the great outdoors. Both sets of grandparents were present, but absent were Jeb and Paul. Jeb recalled being in Maine—and succeeding, finally, in getting to Katahdin on his third try and completing the Appalachian Trail. Paul didn't remember where he was but conceded that the whirlwinds surrounding his brother's death were "beyond the bandwidth of social and emotional skills I had at the time."[31]

The plaque at the north portal to the bridge, erected in the weeks after the dedication, reads:

> BOB BRUGMANN (Feb. 18, 1956-July 4, 1973).
> LOST AT THIS SITE WHILE HIKING THE
> TRAIL HE LOVED. CLARENDON GORGE
> BRIDGE REPLACEMENT SUPPORTED IN
> HIS HONOR BY FAMILY AND FRIENDS

---

31   Distance and life circumstances kept Paul from visiting the bridge until 2023.

Vermont travel publications, hiking books, videos, and blogs I reviewed consistently awarded the gorge high marks for its natural beauty, arresting geology, easy public accessibility, and popularity with visitors, with the suspension bridge itself cited as the feature attraction of the location. Noted less often (and more obliquely) was my friend's drowning. Below are snippets of Clarendon Gorge descriptions, the basic facts in the hiking manuals to chamber of commerce-like gush.

From the GMC's *Long Trail Guide*, 27th edition:

> "Cross the suspension bridge over Mill River. The bridge was built in 1974 to replace a similar structure swept away in the 1973 flood... It is dedicated to the memory of Robert Brugmann."

From the *Appalachian Trail Guide New Hampshire-Vermont*, 12th edition:

> "Originally built in 1974 to replace a similar structure swept away in a 1973 flood, it was refurbished in 2008... It is dedicated to the memory of Robert Brugmann."

From *Exploring the Appalachian Trail: Southern New England*, 2nd edition:

> "If you can't get to Niagara Falls, this gorge will do nicely, though it's quiet and small by comparison... Be careful if you swim below the [suspension bridge]—a 1973 flood took young hiker [Bob Brugmann's] life here."

From *New England Waterfalls*, 3rd edition:

> "What makes [the Clarendon] waterfall special... is the hiker's suspension bridge [which] resides directly above the small cascades and is one of the finest hiker's suspension bridges in New England.

> This gorge is a popular swimming hole with deep yellow/green pools… There are plenty of… large rocks to sit on and bask in the sun."

From "Adventures of Abby Girl" blog:

> "Clarendon Gorge is a must visit place to stop in any season. The suspension bridge is awesome. The gorge is beautiful… If you venture into the rougher or deeper water, make sure you are a strong swimmer."

My own reaction to this location was less effusive. Whereas others call out its beauty and salubrious delights as a party spot, I saw plastic bottle discards bobbing in the water, access paths worn bare from overuse, left behind convenience store lunch detritus, and the specter of violent death.

Tips for gorge visitors: Come on a weekday to avoid crowds. Walk the bridge slowly. Note the force of the river below. Read the commemorative plate. Respectfully remember my friend.

43. The Comeback Trail
Duncannon, Pennsylvania; January 5, 2013

When it comes to career, there are things about my life I'd prefer to let rest. I've been reorganized or downsized out of more organizations than I can count. I've been undervalued, overlooked, kicked around, and, yes, canceled. Multiple times. For the pursuit I think I really had a gift for—coaching college athletes—I was dropped for my alleged "philosophical differences" with my direct report. (That one hurt, badly.) During my thirty-three years of working life, I could confidently name five individuals who, to put it charitably, were heartless bullies; all of whom seemed intent to crush me rather than find ways to work with me and my talents for the betterment of our sectors of humanity. To this day I awaken to at least two "failure" dreams a week.

Do I get angry when I get on this topic?

By 2011, soon after I was "reconfigured" out of a position teaching first-year college writing for which I was a perfect fit, I told friends, "Fuck it, I'm done." I was fifty-five and had had three cardiac ablations. My wife made enough in her corporate post to pay our bills and cover me under her health care benefit. I promised Theresa hair-free bathrooms, shiny countertops, a tidy yard. "Go downtown and make money; milk the company cow while you can," I begged.

Alas, scrubbing the toilets, weeding the gardens, and whiling away good hours accumulating stupid screen time got old. So on a warm January day, I drove an hour forty to Duncannon, jumped on the AT southbound, and hiked seven miles of new trail. Before the end of winter, I returned to the Cove Mountain-Cumberland Valley area of south-central PA three more times, each outing covering four to eight new miles.

Back in 2010, we had a week free in August and looking for something to do. Far enough from home to feel away, close enough not to knock ourselves out going there. I thought about my Appalachian Trail history and identified a mileage gap east of the Hudson River. I plotted a four-day hike across New York to Connecticut, with Theresa dropping me off and picking me up each day at prearranged locations. At night we'd stay at nearby inns and dine out. When I was on the trail by day, she'd explore the area—relax, hike on her own, sip a latte, do anything she wished.

Forty-one miles later, the journey concluded close to where Jeff Gehrs and I passed in 1973. I could now check off New York as my first completed AT state. A seed was planted.

Duncannon is a much-diminished small town near the convergence of two rivers (Juniata, Susquehanna) and four federal highway routes (11, 15, 22, 322). The trail here passes more adult-novelty stores and gentlemen's clubs per mile than anyplace I know on the AT; thru-hikers could tell you that unless this sort of thing is your pastime, Duncannon is not the Shangri-la of the 2,197-mile journey. But at ninety-four miles away, the town was also the location nearest to home to access new AT turf.

It was when I advanced below the Cumberland Valley,

thirty some miles from Duncannon, that I set a goal of completing the AT in Pennsylvania, my home state by adoption. A finished Pennsy, combined with New Jersey and New York from earlier, would give me 387 continuous trail miles and three states. That was only seventeen percent of the whole shebang but maybe enough of a critical mass of trail to incentivize me to keep walking.

Part of the draw of getting back to the AT was the improvement of the route. Back in the days of Bob, Jeb, George Hill, and the scouts, the "trail" across the big valley west of Harrisburg and through the towns east of the Hudson were long road walks best avoided. The worst of the AT. Not anymore. By moving the pathway onto a thin but protected corridor of woods and fields, the updated route successfully threaded through these once problematic places. They were nice hikes, relatively secluded and "out there" in feel—even if I found myself occasionally at the edge of a monster truck terminal or peeking into some trail neighbor's swimming pool.

The task of completing Pennsylvania became easier once Theresa volunteered herself to haul me around to strategic trail-access locations. Now I could hike one way all day and eliminate the need to turn around after lunch and repeat-hike what I just covered back to the car. With Theresa on board as transportation services manager, my new mileage tallies doubled with the same output of energy. By October 2013, ten single-day hikes since Duncannon, I could mark off PA as my third finished state.

I thought I was done with this commuter-style hobby hiking. Except... what's another forty-two-mile dash across skinny Maryland to the Potomac, which I could cover in three days. Would it not make sense to extend my explorations to there, the emotional midpoint of the AT, with trail headquarters across the bridge in Harpers Ferry, West

Virginia? I'd earned, as I checked off Maryland, a stop at Harpers Ferry visitor center, a treasure-trove of AT maps and souvenirs as well as a thru-hiker gathering spot.

On a gentle April day in 2014, during my final Maryland hike, feeling I imagine equal parts satisfied and reflective, my thoughts turned to Bob Brugmann and in a snap moment I hatched yet another plan. I was completing state number four, after NY, PA, and NJ, moving north with the spring on a soft afternoon. Once you get on the AT for a few miles, there's so much to enjoy, I didn't want to stop. The trail just kept going and going and calling one. Hikers know this feeling.

So, what was next? What hadn't I yet tracked on the AT I could yet claim without turning what began as a buffer activity against the ills of retirement ennui into some years-long quest that demanded carrying a full load of camping supplies? What lay beyond Connecticut, which I needed a mere day of hiking to wrap up as my fifth state?

There was of course Massachusetts: ninety delightful Berkshire miles. Then Vermont: arduous ups and down, billions of black flies, and remote. *Was it too ambitious for me to hike everything on the AT to the bridge at Clarendon Gorge, eighty-seven miles north of the Mass-Vermont line, before my sixtieth birthday in July 2016?* I was fifty-seven years old. I'd talk to Theresa and review the maps.

It wasn't easy or free of conflict to dive into something as self-centric as bouncing down a pathway when stuff closer to home was falling apart. My brother, the legendary hitchhiker and man-about-town, was dying. Dad, now past ninety, in decline. Theresa's forever-reliable company paycheck and benefits in the hands of a slippery spinoff. Still, I had an old friend to honor in a way befitting of him. So I pushed on. A couple of days here and there with Theresa providing shuttle services. I finished Mass in the early spring of 2016, two weeks before Ken's own passage through life concluded at age sixty-two.

What J.T. sings about in his best song, "Sweet Baby James," is poetically truthful. The Berkshires were dreamlike; put ten, twenty, or forty miles of them behind you, and upon entering Vermont, there's thousands more miles of mountains—it certainly seemed—to go. I needed nine days of hikes to complete Massachusetts, spread out over seventeen months and four different trips. The AT in the Bay State presented some stiff challenges around Mount Everett and Jug Head in the south, as well as lofty Mount Greylock and a gnarly rock scramble in the final northern miles before slipping into Vermont. In between, it was a mostly low stress walk in the woods; never terribly far from roads and lively towns, yet wild in feel. An ideal set up for an old Jersey boy who could play hard, get dirty, and have fun doing it, but required civilized amenities for overnight recuperation.

44. Green Mountain State
Stamford to Clarendon, Vermont; May 12-July 2, 2016

My love affair with Vermont was woven deep into my biographical and psychological fabric. My first important hike at age 12 was here at Mount Mansfield. My first venture in skiing, Prospect Mountain, at 15. My first college classes and experience in living away from home, Lyndon State, 1974-75. I've rated VT as number-one of the fifty states, ahead of the likes of Washington, Oregon, California, and Colorado, and long considered going there, for any purpose, to be a special occasion.

Less illustriously, Bob Brugmann's Appalachian Trail thru-hike attempt and life ended here near the village of East Clarendon. If I'm to reach the site of my friend's accident ahead of my big six-zero, eighty-six days away, I had to first figure out how to access the footpath. None of my options were easy. Coming at it from the east, Stamford, would upset the nerves some, but I could bang through in a Subaru via a badly potholed dirt road. However, since Theresa and I were staying in Bennington, to the west, we decided to search for the trail from that direction. A sound idea except, in keeping with the state's rugged character, we had to ditch the vehicle and hike the final 2.8 miles up a crude mountain road to reach the AT/LT crossing.

So hiking the trail here, due to its remote location, could be complicated, and I would be max challenged to walk it to the gorge bridge ahead of deadline. My toughest task of all was a 20.6-mile chunk of high-mountain pathway from Route 9 to USFS 71, a logging road inside Green Mountain National Forest. I'd long been away from this level of difficulty in foot travel and hadn't put in this much mileage in a day since my outings with Bob and Jeb in the early seventies. Whatever limber footwork and supple reflexes qualified one as a spring chicken, I'd aged out. But with final pack adjustments and a few sips of water, away I went.

By the end of that marathon day there were moans, groans, and colorful rearrangements of banned words bellowing from inside me. But nine and a half hours after Theresa sent me into the woods with a payload of hydration fluids, lunch, and a netted hat to safeguard my neck and brain from the worst of the bugs, I staggered out—pooped but standing. Pacemaker, blood-thinner meds, gimpy knees and all: I could still do this!

The south end of the state to the Clarendon bridge would require us three trips up from Pennsylvania. And my final four-day effort, beginning June 29, would cover 44.4 miles, starting with a seventeen-mile fanny kicker from Kelley Stand Road to Routes 11 and 30. It was in this dense forest during his attempted 800-mile hike in '72 when health issues forced Bob off the trail and sent him into an extended tailspin. My own walk through here, even during black fly season, was quite pleasurable.

The way I planned it: during my countdown hikes to the gorge I'd tamp down the mileage each day from 17.5 to 12.3 to 8.3 to 6.3. My thinking being more hours to enjoy

Vermont, decreasing labor, and no need to rush on the last day. After some back and forth, I decided to go public with what I was doing here and why.

I was not wild about social media, but when it seemed like I was the last person alive without an online presence, I surrendered the last vestiges of my anonymity to Zuck, stealthy foreign governments, and other nefarious operators and signed on. Ahead of my June 29-July 2 hikes to Clarendon, I announced my intentions and invited the world.

At first, it appeared Jeb would drive down from Canada and walk with me to the bridge. Then three or four HCHS pals piped in: "How wonderful what you're doing, Bruce. I'd love to come with you." Of course, that was idle-time chatter. Who was going to do this hike, even if by AT/LT standards it's a light woodland stroll? People who say yes on social media might be halfway honest in the moment, but few would actually clear out their schedule, rearrange grandparent or pet duties, and road-trip to Vermont during a holiday period to hike with dear old me. Bob was a fondly remembered friend and schoolmate, but 1973 was long ago. People, as I've said, move on.

Citing a family responsibility, Jeb too would bow out. However, he alerted Millie, and let Theresa and I know she'd be driving down from her Connecticut Valley home to meet us.

To drift back decades to that Fourth of July: after Bob arrived at the flood scene, I ask a last time where he was trying to get to that evening that compelled him to attempt the river crossing. We know he was rushing—to catch a bus in two days from Manchester, Jeb said. From Richard Judy, we heard speculation on Bob's possible fixation on keeping a hiking schedule to give him a moonshot chance of reaching Georgia before returning to school. We know from Pam Kerstner that Bob's final trail night was in her family's garage; she's also certain he stayed the night before three miles to the north, at Governor Clement Shelter, having signed the register with a comment on the rain.

After the AT/LT route crosses US 4 at Sherburne Pass, the trail in rapid succession passed Pico Camp, Cooper Lodge, Governor Clement, and finally the Kerstner garage at Lower Cold River Road, in 12.8 miles. Beyond here, it was another four miles to the gorge. Whether Bob slept at Clement or had sequestered at Cooper or Pico, his blitzkrieg pace, in the historic rains, had slowed to a duck-walk. Normally, Bob would cover the US 4 to VT 103 section in a day.

Southbound from Clarendon Gorge, Long Trail shelters were located 2.6 and 7.7 miles ahead. If Bob had settled for the first, even accounting for the bad hiking conditions, that small amount of progress from the Kerstner garage would not satisfy the go-getter kid I knew. A better option, if he could find a little extra oomph, would be to push ahead to the second lean-to in the waning daylight of the early-summer evening. By advancing to Greenwall Shelter, 11.7 miles from the garage, Bob's mileage to the highway to Manchester (Routes 11 and 30) would be cut to 24.6. Which he'd have a day and a half to cover. For Bob, this was manageable.

It's been my experience that a certain subset of goal-motivated hiker, zeroing in on a reward, can find in his/her/their depleted body and brain the mettle to push beyond ordinary limits. As much as these beat-to-pulp warriors seem to thrive on the changing pulse and adversity of the journey, it's the stronger pull of off-trail comforts—a reclining seat on an air-conditioned bus, a bed with clean sheets, a meal or two they're not responsible for cooking, that drive sojourners of Bob's ilk to exceptional feats of perseverance. They love the trail experience, these hardcore types do; but after a month of hardships, these famished foot soldiers crave the comforts of "town life" in any form they could tap.

Of course, any speculation about Bob's ambitions that night in view of what took place at 5:30 is hardly relevant. However, in my final six-mile walk to the Mill River, each step I took was a sharp reminder that my friend never got across the flooded stream. Never hiked this soil. Never made Manchester in time for Friday's New York bus. *Dammit, dammit, dammit!*

◊

From a westerly view known as Airport Lookout, the AT/LT northbound descended a steep 600 feet in three-quarters of a mile. Coming down I first sensed, then heard, then saw the gorge. If Bob's July Fourth holiday hadn't already been a wet and frustrating trudge, the taxing climb out of here while lugging a heavy waterlogged load... well, what more can be said that already hadn't?

The suspension bridge, when I came upon it, extended high over the river. The void below it is a tangle of boulders and channel of swift-running water. While legions blithely gather here to swim and party, I had no interest in the social frivolities or getting near the water knowing what happened here forty-three years before. I couldn't say if the flow that day was high, low, or normal by the seasonal standards of the Mill, but what stood out to me was a sense of danger. It's a lot of liquid, and it's fast. If one were to get trapped down there, an encounter with the rocks could kill. All a bit unsettling to think about in the context of the inundation of early July 1973. This is no place to horse around or take risks.

It was nearly noon on a sunny day when off the south end of the bridge I spotted Theresa with a smallish older woman, who was pointing at something in the stream. I approached and waved.

They arrived earlier, met in the parking area along Route 103, and walked the tenth of a mile down into the gorge, retracing Bob's last steps. Then proceeded across the walkway above the water. The woman with my wife was Millie, the same kind lady who came to my aid that stormy day in Wind Gap—*how long ago, Bruce? Forty-five years!* She, who brought up three boys in difficult circumstances, endured a couple of sputtered marriages, and had weathered four decades of grief.

We exchanged greetings, hugs, and surveyed the scene: a bustle of visitors toting towels and picnic supplies and scatterings of AT/LT hikers hoofing through as they would. Oblivious, of course, to who Bob Brugmann was and the story behind the rustic yet striking bridge here. Millie asked if I preferred my birth name instead of my middle name, which I'd used in my teens. We caught up and reviewed her son's accident. Some things I remembered well, others not at all. We got lunch in a café across 103 and told the staff about Bob's bad luck and my three-year project to hike to Clarendon to honor him.

It was lovely; it was painful. We sobbed.

In a month of high-intensity hiking, Bob had climbed and descended monolithic Katahdin, giant Mount Washington, and a dozen other 4,000 and 5,000 footers. With little trouble. Yet at the trail's second-lowest point in its northernmost 500 miles, the 800-foot Mill River crossing, his hike terminated, and a very promising life was swept away.

Life is great. Then it evens out.

The exceptional confluence of conditions Bob encountered here—bridge gone, gorge flooded, days and days of terrible weather, fatigue, hunger, the pressure he felt to hike more miles, the temptation of a lone tree trunk dangling over the maelstrom as a shortcut across the breach—it's cruel fate all these factors ganged up on my friend in a moment when his vulnerability was elevated and his clarity of thought weakened.

And where, I wanted to know, on this beautiful yet unforgiving earth were the trail angels of mercy, the nuns who had awoken us eleven months before the accident at Sunrise Mountain, when Bob so desperately needed divine intervention?

After eating, Theresa, Millie, and I took a final stroll down to the bridge. I'd turn sixty soon, and it felt good to be on the Appalachian Trail again with one of the family.

◊

Regrettably, I could not invent the miracle Hallmark ending all were rooting for. Only a long overdue love letter to a good friend who enriched my life and the lives of others. Who made one miscalculation, paid the price, and died too young. Whose remarkable story and gut-wrenching final act leaves hearts ajar, and a world stuck as ever in the pincers of an existential crisis with no clear pathway out.

But whose memory will not be lost to the floodwaters of time.

In respect to the living and the deceased, I made the decision to not pursue a copy of Bob's trail journal from the family. Instead, I elected to reconstruct my friend's hike from Katahdin to Clarendon Gorge entirely from documents, maps, memories, and conversations with family and trail companions. If I've misrepresented Bob's intentions or distorted any fact per his journey, I bear full responsibility.

Afterword
Allentown, Pennsylvania; July 2024

Seventeen-thousand nine-hundred and fourteen days after Jeb and I summited Mount Washington, stared into the fog, and moved on, I returned to the mountain. This time Theresa and I arrived the easy way, the cog railway, and basked in the sunshine of a rare cloudless September afternoon. We did what tourists do: look at the other people, the views, and pose for pictures on the rock pile that marks the official high point. Then we poked around the main visitors' building, which housed a cafeteria, gift shop, and museum.

On the right upon entering the building, a small glass-enclosed space serves as the Mount Washington postal station with an active ZIP code: 03589. Just outside this enclosure stood a small, timeworn, blue and red metal mailbox that no doubt now gets little use but was almost certainly the same box where Bob dropped his postcard to me from here ten or eleven days before he was lost to the floodwaters. After all this time I didn't typically lose composure when I talked about July 4, 1973. But when Theresa and I visited Millie four days after our pilgrimage to the mountain and I told her my mailbox story, I broke down.

I've long wondered what Bob was thinking when he wrote in the final line of that postcard: "Maybe you can join me later." This was the card delivered a day or two after the accident. I have a faint memory, from back at school, of Bob talking to me about coming with him on his adventure that summer, presumably for a few days as he passed through lower Pennsylvania, Maryland, maybe northern Virginia. As thus, when Jeb proposed our hike across the Presidential Range in the aftermath of the accident, I felt duty-bound to commit—not only as a friend to the grief-stricken surviving brother, but out of loyalty to the one who died.

I should ask this largely unanswerable question: Would Bob and I have stayed friends into adulthood, even to today (as imagined earlier) had he lived? Or as they did with Jeb and I, would the crosswinds of life cast us apart? Did Bob and I have enough common ground, temperamental and political compatibility to go the distance? Of course, there was no simple answer and maybe no point in attempting to fashion one from posthumous conjecture. So I only pose the question.

My time for hiking Brugmann brothers' style, that summer I turned seventeen, had slithered away. I was building identity in new ways, trying to boost my social position in and out of school to a standard my own brother, Ken Lobb, had established. I was only then, in these weeks before senior year, getting a comfortable handle on teen life. Bob and Jeb, I feared, would kick my tender butt all over the AT if I tried to backpack with them at their aggressive pace. Of course, we know I went to New Hampshire, did fine, loved the White Mountains, and made it back to New Jersey undamaged. And never hiked again with Jeb.

As much as I've doubted myself or thought I've had my fill of hiking, I've stuck with the Appalachian Trail. After

He Was Too Young To Die

I reached the bridge at Clarendon Gorge and reunited with Millie, I kept going. From fall 2016 to 2020, I added 250 miles of Virginia, from the Potomac to south of the James River. Chipping away at my remaining mileage in Vermont, I finished the Green Mountain State in spring 2019. Then a friend egged me into attempting to fill my sixty-two-mile gap between Hanover, New Hampshire, across the Connecticut River from Vermont, and Franconia Notch, where Jeb and I ventured into the core Whites when we were kids on a mission of honor.

As I concluded work on this story, I managed to clamber over the Kinsman Range and close that elusive New Hampshire mileage gap south and west of Franconia. In the coming years I hope to tie up some loose ends in Virginia near the famed McAfee Knob and bring the southern reach of my AT history to past Great Smoky Mountains National Park and into Georgia: my fourteenth and final state. But tally it all up, and I've barely passed the fifty-percent mark. That's everything logged in fifty-four years, including eight completed states: Vermont, Massachusetts, Connecticut, New York, New Jersey, Pennsylvania, Maryland, and West Virginia. That's a long sweep of AT, but only a humbling halfway to royalty. To think that determined thru-hikers do in two and a half months what's taken me four-fifths of my life: that too is humbling.

I admire the thru-hikers, honestly, even if I'd grumble now and then that they're (stereotypically) a technology-consumed bunch of advantaged kids; or grow weary of the trail-name culture so sacrosanct to them. I like reading about their bold, funny, and endearing exploits in the substantial body of published AT literature—some of which is wonderful, and some sorely in need of spellcheck and professional editing. When I meet them on the trail, they're an endlessly curious and colorful sight, upbeat, engaging. What I've assembled in these pages is one more variation of a thru-hiker story. But more accurately, a friendship story with an AT thru-hiking angle.

To say it a final time: I'm not a thru-hiker type, never was. But I'm a devoted Appalachian Trail enthusiast who'll continue to snag new mileage anywhere the currents of life lead me, for as long as my health allows. Onward and upward!

Truths of the Trail

Collected from five and a half decades of hiking up and down the AT, here are eleven essential Truths of the Trail to keep in mind before setting out for an hour or a 2,197-mile trip of a lifetime.

1. Never put a daily distance quota or destination goal ahead of personal safety considerations.
2. Be watchful of any potential hazard. Accidents happen when you don't expect them to.
3. There are easy miles and easy hours along the trail, but few easy days. If you've enjoyed a mellow morning, expect to pay dues in sweat, rough terrain, and ascent in the afternoon.
4. No matter how many miles a day one knocks out, peaks one claims, or vertical feet one collects, other hikers will claim more in miles, peaks, or vertical. They'll also have snazzier gear and slicker technology. Accept it and don't try to out-compete these super-hikers.

5. Each mile hiked late in the day feels like two miles. Sometimes, three.
6. If you see mountains ahead, you soon will climb into them, not go around or away from them.
7. Where there's the option of a shorter or longer route to a summit, the shorter option will be the harder.
8. There are no absolutes when it comes to anticipated trail conditions, weather, or estimated hiking times. Plan accordingly.
9. The popular conception that the AT is overcrowded is, with a few exceptions, overstated.
10. Electronic navigational devices are now standard equipment. They are phenomenally useful in recording distance, marking location and route, tallying elevation change, and measuring other good stuff such as moving speed. Hikers check their progress on them incessantly; then they compare and debate the numbers they yield. Fewer hikers now rely on paper maps. But maps are simple to transport, add welcome estimation and surprise to a hike, need no recharging, and are works of art in themselves.
11. You can still get lost. Be attentive to trail markings and have a general understanding of your intended direction of travel. Should you not see a marker at a reliable interval, or sense something about your route is amiss, stop. Turn around and retrace your steps to the last clearly identifiable marker. Then look for the correct continuation of the trail.

Trail Talk

References to various trails, some hiking jargon, and a few useful acronyms appear throughout these pages. For those less acquainted with the Appalachian and other trails, outdoor organizations, and land protection/management agencies important to our story, here are sketches of who and what they are and what they do.

Trails & Trail-Support Entities:

Appalachian Trail (AT) The celebrated fourteen-state footpath from Springer Mountain, Georgia, to Baxter Peak, Maine (more familiarly known as Katahdin). Completed, 1937; current length, 2,197.3 miles.

Appalachian Trail Conservancy (ATC) The administrative arm for the management of the Appalachian Trail, for its owner, the National Park Service. Known as Appalachian Trail Conference prior to 2005. Located along the trail route in Harpers Ferry, West Virginia.

Appalachian Mountain Club (AMC) Venerated

outdoor and conservation organization dating to 1876; instrumental in establishing New Hampshire's White Mountains as a global hiking destination. The AMC built, staffs, and maintains the famed White Mountains huts for overnight hikers. Via a wide-ranging network of chapters, activities, and facilities in support of self-propelled recreation, Boston-based AMC extends from New England to Virginia.

Adirondack Park/Adirondack Mountain Club (ADK) The widely used ADK abbreviation for "all things" Adirondack is applicable to the giant northern New York park and forest preserve, as well as to the group that manages its trails and regulates hiker use. The ADK club dates to 1922 and sponsors the popular 46er program, which recognizes individuals who climb all the park's forty-six peaks of 4,000 feet and higher.

Green Mountain Club (GMC) The GMC has built and sustained Vermont's hiking trails (most notably, the Long Trail) since 1903. Responsible for shelters and infrastructure for the state's 100-mile joint Long Trail/Appalachian Trail corridor, including the Bob Brugmann Footbridge at Clarendon Gorge.

Long Trail (LT) The north-south Vermont footpath that spans the length of the state, Quebec to Massachusetts. Completed in 1931; length, 272 miles. The LT follows the Green Mountain chain and is recognized as the prototype for an emergent Appalachian Trail during the 1920s and 1930s.

Federal Parks & Land-Protection/Management Agencies:

Delaware Water Gap National Recreation Area (DWGNRA) The 70,000-acre property alongside the Delaware River created in the 1970s from condemned lands after the defeat of the Tocks Island dam. This park provides a ridgeline corridor for twenty-five miles of the New Jersey AT.

National Park Service (NPS) Agency responsible for 428 parks, historic sites, monuments, preserves, and other special properties throughout the fifty states and territories. As a designated National Scenic Trail, the Appalachian Trail qualifies as a unit of the NPS system and receives government support and protection. However, most AT administrative functions are performed by the quasi-independent ATC in Harpers Ferry, including trail maintenance by hiking club volunteers. In many locations, NPS-acquired buffer lands enable a safeguarded AT to successfully traverse developed areas.

United States Forest Service (USFS) Agency responsible for all U.S. national forest lands, seven units of which host AT mileage, including White Mountain and Green Mountain National Forests.

Trail Talk II: Who's Who

How do you distinguish an Appalachian Trail thru-hiker from a section hiker or end-to-end hiker? It can be confusing. The descriptions below for the most common classifications of AT hikers should help clarify who's who on the trail.

Thru-Hiker As designated by ATC, any foot traveler who completes all 2,197 unique miles of the Appalachian Trail within a one-year period.

Section Hiker Any shorter-duration hiker out for a period of days, a week, or multiple weeks covering up to hundreds of miles. Should a section hiker eventually finish the full trail, he/she/they are entitled to claim **End-to-End Hiker** status, even if their efforts to cover the full trail take decades.

Day Hiker This cohort of trail user may carry a full pack, use trekking poles and tally some respectable stats by day's end. But no day hiker sleeps in the woods: in a tent, hammock, lean-to shelter, or cabin without modern plumbing, linens, and an electrical outlet. This is your classic AT day hiker, or motel hiker. This is me.

Our Old School

Located in Flemington, New Jersey, Hunterdon Central High School opened in 1956. The HCHS acronym familiar to my generation and used here now includes an "R" for Regional: HCRHS. The school district of 160 square miles is one of the largest in the state; it encompasses small towns, suburban landscapes, farms, and boondocks roughly midway between New York and Philadelphia. Current enrollment grades 9 through 12 is around 2,600. Bob Brugmann and I were members of the school's Class of 1974.

Acknowledgements

Nearly everybody I asked from the Brugmann/Curtis family, old school friends, or people from the Appalachian Trail and Long Trail communities whose lives intersected with Bob's enthusiastically offered me their time, memories, and insights during the development of this project. Their contributions enabled me to turn a fuzzy story idea anchored by fifty-year-old journal entries, newspaper clippings, and fragmented memories into a more dynamic and more complete work. For especially those in Bob's family who put their faith in me, which required of them extra strength and a revisit to a painful time, thank you. I am most grateful.

A good friend, Lisa Hamm-Greenawalt, shot the author photo and several other striking images from Clarendon Gorge that unfortunately did not make it into the book. Lisa is an author, journalist, and blogger. She is a seasonal resident of Ludlow, Vermont.

Through their own perseverance, two authors provided me the inspiration and staying power to bring this project to completion. Rick Bylina, one of my oldest friends, is the creator of four novels, a memoir, a volume of short fiction, and a book of poetry. Decades past at college in Mansfield, Pennsylvania, Rick talked about his dream of writing and publishing novels; later on, he fulfilled that dream. Learn about Rick's books and world of words at https://rickbylina.com. Rick also generously read this book's early manuscript and offered valuable editorial, publication, and marketing insights. Ken Lobb, my late brother, repackaged his 1971 New Jersey-to-California hitchhiking trip into *We Picked Up*, a splendid novelization of that trip that he published in 2014. Ken and Rick both spent many years weaving their ideas into impressive works of literature. I am indebted to both.

However, without the confidence, cajoling, and (tender and tough) love of my wife of thirty-one years, Theresa Oravec, I could not have taken this project to the finish line. Terry has been my ace in the trenches since the beginning. She has served at various times as my research assistant, IT lifeline, copy cop, chauffer to trailheads down terrible roads, advisor, and cheerleader. And, anytime I might whine or whimper, my drill sergeant. She's awesome!

Finally, to the staff at Onion River Press in Burlington, Vermont, who took a chance on this first-time author from outside their region and enthusiastically guided him through multiple revisions to the finish line, I owe you a hug. In the year from when you accepted me into your lineup of jobs to publication, your helpful suggestions have enabled me to pull together a worthy book that tells a worthy story. Rachel Fisher, Riley Earle, Sofia Silva Wright, and Rachel Carter, thank you!

About the Author

Welles Bruce Lobb began journaling in seventh grade in 1969 and hiking the Appalachian Trail in his birth state of New Jersey a year later. He holds bachelor's degrees from Mansfield University and Cedar Crest College, both in Pennsylvania, and worked as a news reporter, magazine editor, freelance writer, higher education PR professional, and college writing instructor for thirty-three years. He additionally served as an intercollegiate cross-country and track coach for twenty years and remains a life mentor to many. Welles lives with his wife, Theresa Oravec, in Allentown, Pennsylvania, and seeks new trail and travel adventures anywhere the winds and tides of life take him. This is his first book.

Milton Keynes UK
Ingram Content Group UK Ltd.
UKHW030959080824
446563UK00004B/242